2.60

.50

The Dell War Series

The Dell War Series takes you onto the battlefield, into the jungles, and beneath the oceans with unforgettable stories that offer a new look at the terrors and triumphs of America's war experience. Many of these books are eye-witness accounts of the duty-bound fighting man. From the intrepid foot soldiers, sailors, pilots, and commanders, to the elite warriors of the Special Forces, here are stories of men who fight because their lives depend on it.

☆ ☆ ☆ ☆ ☆ ☆ ☆

D0696592

BATTLE AT DONG TRE

Roberts had slipped and fallen into a cleft halfway up the bank. He was now standing and yelling: "Give us smoke!" More red was thrown, and this time some green.

Under its cover, Roberts moved to get Denson, under the impression that the sergeant was still alive. Discovering his mistake, he still pulled out rearward, dragging the body.

Then Roberts started back for Cromer, though bullets were kicking up dirt all around him.

Together, Housley and Calvert crawled forward, also pointing for Cromer. They could hear Cromer yelling: "God damn it, don't forget me. Don't leave me out here."

Housley called: "Don't worry, we're coming to get you."

Roberts was now walking boldly up the trail, acting like a man who didn't care to live very long, blasting with his M-16 as he moved. . . .

S· L· A· MARSHALL

THE

FIELDS OF BAMBOO

DONG TRE, TRUNG LUONG and HOA HOI
Three Battles Just Beyond the South China Sea

Field Sketches by Mark Lennox and the Author

A DELL BOOK

Published by
Dell Publishing
a division of
Bantam Doubleday Dell Publishing Group, Inc.
666 Fifth Avenue
New York, New York 10103

ISBN: 0-440-21209-X

Reprinted by arrangement with The Battery Press

Printed in the United States of America

Published simultaneously in Canada

March 1992

10 9 8 7 6 5 4 3 2 1

RAD

THE
FIELDS OF BAMBOO

CONTENTS

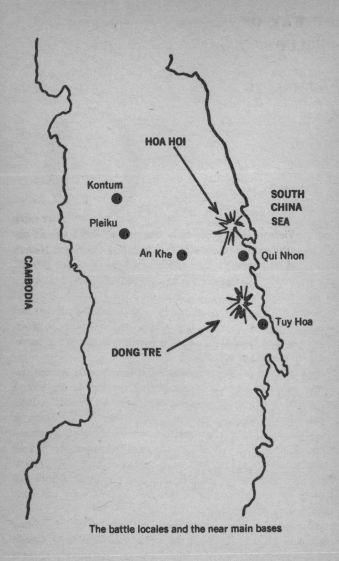

The battle locales and the near main bases

BY WAY OF PRELUDE

ON MY THIRD tour in Vietnam during the early summer of 1966 I was an observer-participant in the battle that is called Operation Nathan Hale, and on my fourth tour which lasted the winter of 1966–67 my official duties required me to get a full and final accounting of what had happened on that field.

It was done by assembling the survivors of every unit that had fought, interviewing them as a group, and recording their experiences personal and in common from the beginning of movement till the end of fighting.

This method of reconstructing what develops in combat, relating cause to effect, and eliminating the fog, is my own. I pioneered it during the invasion of the Gilbert Islands in 1943, and thereafter applied it during World War II and Korea. It works because it is simple and because what one man remembers will stir recall in another. The one inviolable rule, if such group interviewing is to get valid results, is that the question-and-answer routine must be in sequence step-by-step from first to last. Of my experience in this line of field work came my calls to duty in Vietnam.

All memory is tricky, none more so than that of the fighting man, with his need to forget the worst of it. Whether we could get a dependable response from Nathan Hale survivors was a main question. Before then, the most protracted group interviewing had been in connection with the Omaha Beach landings in June 1944, the book on which had been finally closed in September, four months later. Six months had elapsed since the battle when I began working with the Nathan Hale participants in early December 1966. To my gratification, the troopers could still recall vividly and accurately what had been done and said. That I had reconned the whole zone of operations from a Huey piloted by Major General Jack Norton, commander of the First Cavalry Division (Airmobile), had made several touch downs for personal interviewing, and completed my sketches while the ground was hot, perforce gave me a rounded familiarity with the campaign and stimulated the response. I was not a stranger.

The events of that field would otherwise be lost to the national history. Operation Nathan Hale was so little regarded that it does not receive mention in the book *Report on the War in Vietnam*, the distinguished authors of which are Admiral U. S. Grant Sharp and General W. C. Westmoreland.

The other Vietnam campaign of which I write here, only in part, followed Nathan Hale by three months, and once again the cavalry division was the main fighting body. Begun early in September, this campaign is formally called Operation Thayer-Irving, though the fighters and their commanders who participated in it would like to forget the Thayer portion, which came first. Operation Thayer's details are excluded from this work for much the same reason. The campaign was incredibly boring, wasteful, and exhausting. Rarely in warfare has so much heavy artillery been brought up to shoot at clay pipes. Operation Thayer was a bust. Operation Irving, which swiftly followed, was an unexpected and spectacular success. So the two names were linked together, thereby partly to redeem the whole by implying that all along the hounds had been on the trace.

We have here in Thayer-Irving a phenomenon that is recurrent in operations against irregular forces though uncommon in conventional war. The surprises are constant and the too-frequent ambushing, though always painful and embarrassing, is the lesser part of them. However sedulous the collecting and collating of intelligence by our field force may be, the realities of a situation that can be developed only by hitting are rarely, if ever, what one went forth expecting to find.

The sure thing proves to be an empty bag. The seeming flash-in-the-pan turns into a major explosion. Elephant guns are used to bang away at rabbits. Tigers are hunted with popguns.

Thayer and Irving taken together are prime illustrations of the point. In the one there was a tremendous windup that led only to a demoralizing letdown. In the other, a fluke shot into a bush killed a grizzly.

When Jack Norton deployed major forces of the First Cavalry Division into the Kim Son, Soui Ca, and 506 valleys in September 1966, there was full reason to believe that the search-and-destroy mission would bag big game. These three valleys were known to be solid Viet Cong country. The cavalry had probed them in hit-and-run excursions on numerous occasions and had invariably struck fire. The Soui Ca and Kim Son, although G2 did not at this time know it, served as the supply base of the Second VC Regiment.

These valleys are all good rice-growing country. There is much description of the Soui Ca and the Kim Son in my two books, *Bird* and *Battles in the Monsoon,* which need not be repeated here. The 506, a vale with well-tended fields and paddies laid out in charming geometric patterns, is the fairest of them all. The farms are set apart by neatly manicured hedgerows and the palm groves and orchards are more spacious than elsewhere in the province.

Norton's aim in launching the campaign was to prevent the rice crop from the coastal part of Binh Dinh Province from falling into enemy hands. The obvious and only way to do it was to work over each of the three valleys systematically. There was every reason to believe that at this season the Viet Cong, if not the NVA, would be sticking around home base in force. Or so the campaign planners figured.

The launch was made on 7 September and the greater part of two brigades of the First Cavalry Division was placed either at bat, on deck, or in the hole.

Next day came the news indicating that the movement would not only prove fruitful but also had been exquisitely timed.

The Phu Ly bridge, across the Soui Ca River, is one of the most sensitive points along Highway No. 1, which parallels the east coast and stays just as close to the South China Sea as the stubborn facts of geography permit. On the night of 8 September 1966, it was being guarded by a platoon of Vietnamese Popular Force soldiers. That was far too little strength to beat back an attack by a force of North Vietnamese regulars estimated at two battalions, which came at the bridge's northern abutments from two directions. By luck a column of the 41st ARVN Regiment had just started to cross the bridge when the attack started. With their help, the seizure of the bridge was thwarted and the attackers withdrew toward the northeast. The incident indicates that guerrilla intelligence is not always inspired.

The cavalrymen, already in movement, were redeployed to the north and northeast to close all serviceable escape routes, as revealed by the map. Operation Thayer, named after West Point's contribution to the National Hall of Fame, had opened on a wing and a prayer and it already looked as if the prayer had been answered.

In the end nothing worth writing about came of it. Many went forth to seek and in the aggregate found so little that their sweat and worry will go unnoted in history. Either the enemy was not there or, if present, was so adroit and clever that American genius and aggressiveness must be rated as something less than we believe.

I have about twenty thousand words on Operation Thayer, almost none of which would add anything important to either this writing or an analyst's view of what the Vietnamese bush fighters are like. Our people went, they saw, and they concurred that they had done little and learned less from the campaign. It was an exercise in frustration, an ultimate test of combat morale when soldiers know they are wearing out their jungle boots and their bodies while risking malaria, the bite of the bamboo viper, attack by a man-eating tiger, and the rancor of their leaders—which is perhaps the sorriest hazard of all—to do nothing that common sense says is truly worthwhile.

Numerous rice caches were found and either destroyed or let alone because the task of ruin or removal was not possible with the force present.

Not a few pigs were killed. Cows fared better for a while because they could be driven out over the distance required to end up in the stomach of a South Vietnamese refugee.

One large rice cache was fed into the Soui Ca River. The rice swelled. It formed a dam. The dam began to flood the valley. Demolitions were applied to break the dam.

Old men, old women, and little children would appear, be given such help as was needed, and then later evacuated to a refugee camp, if they so chose. One fifty-six-year-old woman was later found to be the chief VC recruiter in her village.

Viet Cong, singly or in pairs, would shoot from cover and then run for the rear. Now and then a GI would get killed because he happened to be in the way of a bullet rather than because of true aim. Singly, or sometimes in pairs, Viet Cong got killed in much the same way.

Some arms caches were located. None was of such size that its seizure justified the effort to take it over. The search was thorough enough; the loot just wasn't there.

At times, bodies of the enemy would be seen, in platoon size or larger, khaki-clad or in black pajamas. Invariably, the sighting would be at distance. Before the Americans could close, the enemy force would have vanished into thin air.

Leads that in retrospect looked promising did indeed appear. Sometimes they went unrecognized until after the opportune moment had passed. At other times darkness fell too quickly, the force at hand was not sufficient to deal with the target, there was too little lift to bring in other units, and so the brigade commander called it all off.

The South Vietnam national election coincided with the start of Operation Thayer, further complicating the problem of the First Cav. Its main object was to back up and buck up the ARVN. Still, the Cav had to deploy soldiers to help protect the polling places. They were instructed that, if sniped at, they would simply seek protection; to multiply the number of bullets buzzing about would too greatly compound the strain on the voters.

Operation Thayer did not make sense to the soldiers who dealt with its stresses for almost one month. How then could others possibly get it in perspective? In the course of the operation, many men spent their energy in vain endeavor. A few died. Quite a few more were wounded. The Division's losses from malaria and accidental wounds became more grievous. Hueys and overland transport took a beating. The price of poker went up. But one can no more say that the operation was foolish than one can call Operation Irving, which swiftly followed, a stroke of genius. Both were according to the nature of the problem, which no fighting man may understand fully, though it is a kiddies' game for Senators Kennedy and Fulbright and other experts.

Enough to sum up by saying that while good things came of the election, practically nothing good came of Operation Thayer which was going on at the same time. They were in marked contrast even when measured in the unpleasant terms of targets hit and bodies counted. The few dramatic incidents of the period and the small number of productive contacts built up around the polling places, with Charlie trying to come in close enough to scare the voters away from the balloting booths and the Americans running interference for the South Vietnamese who accepted the risk.

Though reporting on the election is not the purpose at hand, some of the happenings of the day make lively reading. A cavalry unit captured intact a Viet Cong propaganda squad with nine players, one of them a woman. All were musicians and entertainers. In this guise they would gain entrée to a village, stage their act, win friends and influence people, and later welcome the little fishes into their gently smiling jaws. What makes this worth passing along was a comment by one of the players: "We are a little Bob Hope show."

At Tan Ohai, an ARVN platoon was moved into a school yard to secure it for a later landing that day by a cavalry unit. They formed a perimeter, only to be pulled out four hours later because of a change in plan. While the choppers were carrying them away amid a heavy downpour, two VC companies came on, charging toward the school yard. Because of the storm, they had missed seeing the extraction. The ARVN artillery, called on just in time, bombarded the school yard. The TOT zapped this formation dead on. Nevertheless, school yard violence is less common in Vietnam than in the U.S.

There are a thousand and one such juicy tidbits concerning the Cav and the election. Regarding month-long Operation Thayer, one searches for the same almost in vain. It was the big sweep to end all big sweeps, though it didn't. There is neither epic tragedy nor comic relief. Point is more lacking than plot. Hence it cannot be divided into acts and no one scene, taken by itself, stands serious examination.

We might cite one example.

The curtain has just risen.

The chopper-borne parties are hunting for suitable landing zones.

One observer sees just what the doctor ordered. From a hundred feet above he sees a flat, elephant-grass-covered field large enough to allow ten Hueys to set down at one time. He estimates the grass to be three to four feet high. The chopper lowers and hovers just above the top of the grass. The observer drops off, falls twelve feet, and breaks a leg.

The elephant grass stands ten feet high and more. The field is on three different levels, and the tallest grass, standing twice as tall as a man, is on the lowest level. Nature has played a trick on man, an outright deception: The grass has topped off as evenly as a field of Dakota wheat. The ground surface is so rough that at most only two Hueys may put down at one time.

Is this tragic, comic, or plain boring?

To the man with the broken leg it was probably all of these things, though no one likes to take a beating from a sea of grass.

Operation Thayer is written off, not because it is exactly a cipher, but because nothing concerning it is truly illuminating except the one simple and solemn fact—with fighting troops the nonfight afield is more tedious, more nerve-wearing, and more exasperating than doing latrine police in an otherwise cushy billet.

For the First Cavalry Division, Operation Thayer was a demoralizer. By the end, failure had gone to the heads of officers and ranks. The Division claimed to have killed 221 Charlies and bagged 72 more in three weeks of campaigning. Also entered on the boxscore were 107 tons of VC rice, but none of salt.

Too bad.

The troopers needed more than a grain of the latter commodity if those figures were to be swallowed.

So the Division faced toward the China Sea. There was a strip along the coastal flank that had not been beaten out. To secure this strip would be the goal of Operation Irving.

Nothing was expected of this operation, named to honor the creator of Ichabod Crane, and no less the Headless Horseman. The show started in the spirit of the latter; it was performed merely in the interests of tidying up. What came of the odds-against gamble that followed the sure thing that failed to pan out is told only in part in these pages. Hoa Hoi was only the beginning. At the finish the Division had eliminated, in one way or another, more than one thousand of the enemy.*

There must be a lesson here of a kind not to be drawn by a shavetail tactician or the JCS. It's the stuff of James Otis and Horatio Alger. Up the slope. Never say die. Bound to win. If at first you don't succeed, try, try again. Persistence is not counted among the military virtues. Yet much must be said for it.

---

* The First Cavalry Division claim sheet for Operation Irving was itemized as follows: enemy soldiers KIA (by body count), 681; possible additional KIA, 128; POW count, 220; civilian defendants (VC supporters rounded up), 1,172; individual weapons taken, 191; crew-served weapons, 19; small arms ammo captured, 377,417 rounds; TNT in pounds, 350; mines, 226; grenades; medical supplies, 2,000 lbs.; telephones, 6; radios, 3; rice, 66.6 tons; salt, 496.2 tons.

DARKNESS AT
DONG TRE

THE NEWLY ARrived captain was both perfectly composed and more than a little bit on edge, the inward churning and the outward calm making him no different from the two intelligence sergeants with whom he was talking things out, though they had been long in the country.

The place: Dong Tre, a Special Forces camp a short piece inland from the port of Tuy Hoa on Vietnam's east coast.

The time: Sunset on 17 June 1966, a clear day on which one could see less than forever.

"Dong Tre," one of the sergeants had said, "means bamboo field."

It seemed unlikely. There was no bamboo within eyesight.

Their problem was one of having too much to do in too little time, a not uncommon bind in irregular warfare as in the daily doings of an average housewife.

Captain Allan James Holmes had arrived two days before to take command of SF Team A-222, and Captain Robert Koerdas, who knew the territory very well, had promptly—all too promptly—left on another assignment. Koerdas had been at Dong Tre six months.

Holmes had spent his two days meeting the people and inspecting the entrenched camp, making suggestions for improvement as he moved about. There was much room for improvement. Some of the defensive wire was beaten down and badly rusted, and though the trenches were well sited some of the walls had collapsed under the monsoon rain.

Now on his third evening, following the dinner hour, Holmes was sitting with the two sergeants to hear what they could tell him about the enemy situation.

A thirty-year-old native New Mexican, born in Anthony, next to the Texas border, and educated at New Mexico State in nearby Las Cruces, Holmes is a man not easily jolted. Yet what he heard from SFC Ted Nixon, the senior intelligence hand, almost pulled him out of his chair.

"Somewhere out there," said Nixon, waving a hand toward the north and east, "are at least two NVA regiments, and maybe three independent VC battalions."

Though Holmes had never heard such talk before, he replied with seeming calm: "Well, what about it?" He half suspected Nixon was testing his reactions.

Nixon answered, "This is a new situation, I mean the concentration. So I figure an attack is coming very fast. We're almost sure of it from what our agents tell us."

Holmes asked: "What's the target?"

Said Nixon, "They'll either hit this camp or hit La Hai, the district capital."

Again a question from Holmes: "How much time have we got?"

Said Nixon, "I'd say at most three days."

At that point, Nixon's assistant, SFC Tommy Tucker, broke in with these words: "Put me down as saying it's more likely to be one week."

Holmes asked: "Why do you figure that way?"

Tucker explained his theory: "Charlie is still doing a lot of digging around out there, though we don't know why. That's what the boys tell us. Our agents around here are mainly wood gatherers. The most dependable one is the fellow we call Long Key. He averages about seventy per cent accurate. We expect him in tomorrow. That's routine. If the heat was on, he'd come in sooner. I'd wait until Long Key gets here before sounding any alarm."

Tucker's cheerful tone made it sound as if either hurrying or taking any extra precaution would be beneath dignity.

Holmes had heard more than enough, however, to conclude otherwise. The camp would not be hit that night, he told himself, the wish being father to the thought. Even so, the position was too undermanned to take any risks beyond that time.

Holmes got on the radio telephone to Major Raymond George, the chief of SF Team B-22, which was based in the center of An Khe village, an hour's run by chopper to the north. Holmes said to him: "This camp must be reinforced just as quickly as possible."

George listened patiently to Holmes's sad story, and though he discounted it more than half, there being no corroboration of the information from other sources, he said in the end: "We'll see that you get what you need, but we can't do much for you tonight."

After Holmes rang off, the three men at Dong Tre talked on for another hour, the two sergeants this time going over the friendly situation with the new captain. What Holmes heard was not calculated to put his mind at ease.

To the northeast of Dong Tre are three hills; the nearest one is three "klicks" (kilometers) from the base camp, the farthest is seven. Insignificant in height and almost barren of vegetation, they are conspicuous only because of the flatness of the surrounding plain.

The command mission at Dong Tre was to keep secure the main road running from the base to La Hai, and this road was flanked by the three hills. Accordingly, three platoons from the garrison were outposting the hills, an assignment that left less

LA HAI

TRUNG LUONG

C.I.D.G.
ENTRENCHED
HILLS

Launched between the special forces
camps at Dong Tre and La Hai,
the battle spread from the entrenched
hills eastward to the village of
Trung Luong

DONG TRE

than one company of Vietnamese to man the trenches of the base camp.

No American had gone along with the three outguarding platoons.

A sorrier scattering of strength would have been hard to devise.

Holmes said: "We're loose as a goose and it's too late to do anything about it. So we take a chance. Everybody sleeps but the two guards on the main gate."

Feeling no real alarm, Holmes hit the sack.

Somewhere around 2100 the three platoons to the northeast called in. All was quiet. The eight six-man ambushes that had been strung along the road and trails west of the hills had bagged nothing. That way from Dong Tre the countryside is mainly wide open, rather barren, with no jungle and little natural cover—no playground in which to monkey about in the dark.

The night was clear, starlit, and still, with not a breath of air stirring. At 0145 (18 June) a Vietnamese Special Force soldier, called an LLDV, who, watchful and wakeful, had been tuning in on the outpost company for the fun of it, said to the guard on the gate: "Funny, I suddenly lose all contact with them. Wonder why?"

The guard did nothing about this rather startling development, and the eager hand with the radio, having passed along the information, lost interest in the subject and retired for the night.

For that lapse, both men may be forgiven. Unlike the Americans they had no knowledge of menace close at hand and loss of contact by RT at midnight may signal only sleepiness at the switch.

At 0200 the gate guard saw flares flash on the nighest hill.

At 0215 the same guard who had fluffed off the man with the radio decided at last it was time to act. He routed Holmes out of bed, saying: "Come quick and look. Something funny going on up there."

Up and out in an instant, Holmes, clad only in his shorts, stood listening. He heard four distinct and quite loud explosions from the direction of the three hills. There followed a prolonged volleying of automatic fire in the northeast. It was astounding how distinctly the sounds carried over distance in the still night air.

Holmes switched on his own PRC-25.

He was just in time to catch the voice of the commander of Third Platoon of the embattled company saying: "Under full attack, grenades, satchel charges, machine guns. Running out of ammunition. We got many bodies stacked up."

Surprisingly, the voice sounded steady enough.

Within a few seconds, and before Holmes could make a move, he heard the voice of Lieutenant Thuan, the Viet boss at the base camp, cut in, talking at such a clip that nothing he said was intelligible.

Holmes ran straight for Thuan, shouting: "Tell them to break contact at once! Tell them to get the hell off those hills! Tell them to head for here!"

Thuan tried. The call didn't roger. All communication had ceased with the last words that had been heard by Holmes.

For one moment Holmes felt an agony of depression and dullness.

Then, still wearing only his shorts, he ran outside again to have another look. Green star clusters were burning above the two nearest hills. To Holmes, they looked exactly like United States-issue lights.

Too, the sounds of the fire exchange in the northeast seemed to be tapering off. Putting these two signs together, Holmes felt a short surge of hope. For the last time, he tried to raise the outpost force on his PRC-25. Nothing came back to him.

There was no longer room for doubt. The hills had been taken and if any friendlys survived, they must be heading for Dong Tre.

The real question was whether the attack on the hills was an isolated incident or the opening ploy of the big show that Nixon had seen coming.

Holmes turned back to Thuan, saying to him: "It's time for you to get the reaction company on the road."

Thuan said, "Sorry, sir, absolutely no."

Holmes said, "You must do it. There isn't any time to lose."

Thuan shook his head, then said in a very low voice: "Sorry, very sorry, but no movement till first light."

"You will."

"I will not."

"You must."

"I must not."

So they argued back and forth. Thuan wouldn't budge an inch. Holmes, wholly baffled, put in a call to Major George at An Khe. George, somewhat groggy from sleep, told him to put Thuan on the RT.

George said to him, "I tell you that you better get out there now."

Holmes, listening hard, said nothing.

Thuan answered quietly, "No move till first light. Very sorry."

George said to Holmes, "I think there'll be no movement till first light."

At that point Holmes gave up, though he fixed Thuan with a look that would spike a gun. Resentful, disgusted, the New Mexican nevertheless kept his temper, and though he cussed a bit, it was under his breath. Not merely the proprieties but the ground rules in this strangely tandemized command arrangement kept him in check. He was not a chief but only an adviser. Thuan was his junior in age and rank. He thought Thuan was reacting out of cowardice.

Still, Thuan smiled, spoke softly, and acted steady as a rock. The pieces didn't fit.

Holmes asked, "And you are sure you are right?"

Thuan answered with a grin, "Sure. We move at first light."

Luckily, in that moment the certainty in the Vietnamese begot an ungrudging respect in the American. Though Holmes was acting strictly on hunch in going along with Thuan, his hunch paid off. Later, he could look back and give thanks that Thuan's obduracy had saved the command and stopped him from making a fatal blunder.

The Westerner had much too quickly concluded that speed of reaction was all, everything. The Oriental was convinced that the Dong Tre garrison was the real target and that the enemy would be waiting outside, set for ambush in great strength.

Though not a large camp, Dong Tre would still have the spread of three fairly large city blocks. The defensive works, trenches, and wire entanglements mainly, though crude and indifferently maintained, were sufficient for the two companies. The enemy would hardly dare put them under siege. The American bases at An Khe and Tuy Hoa were much too close, and already the First Cavalry Division and one battalion of the 327th (101st Division's First Brigade) were getting the word of a rising storm next to Dong Tre.

Holmes considered, then called Major George to say: "We must have air support. Will you see that it is on station by 0600?"

George promised that it would be.

Then Holmes and Thuan sat down to do their planning. The garrison was awakened and pulled from bed, to be ready for breakfast by 0400. It would take quite some time to get the rice pots boiling.

Holmes and Thuan agreed that one column would be marched straight across the rice paddies to the northeast, striking for the first hill, which was about twenty meters higher than the other two. The other command would entruck and move via the road for the farthest hill, seven klicks distant. Its movements from that point would depend upon developments.

Holmes said: "Once we start, we move just as fast as possible."

Thuan nodded, expressionless, as if he were thinking of something else.

When first light came, at about 0615, as the marching company started through the main gate, the first fugitives from the night action began coming in. They were a sorry lot, half-clad, dirty, many of them bleeding badly, all of them bubbling with scare stories, few of which were reconcilable. This is the usual thing. But one theme was recurrent. "More than a hundred VC hit us on each hill."

Holmes by this time was ready to believe. He was not coping with some small hit-and-run affair, a raid or anything of the sort, but the opening of a major action.

Even the sight of the runaways gave him a bit of a shock. Two-thirds of them were naked or wearing only a loincloth; all were scratched from head to heel from having run through thorn bushes. None wore shoes and not one had come out with a weapon. The arms had been thrown away at the start of mad flight.

As they regained their wind and some confidence born of an awareness that they were for the moment in safe haven, some bravado returned. They began boasting about the fierce resistance they had put up for almost an hour.

Holmes said to Thuan: "They're lying. They were caught asleep and stampeded by surprise. There was no real fire fight. You can look at them and see what has happened."

Thuan nodded.

Holmes continued: "So we better hold up the movement. Those hills are certain to be loaded. And besides, we still don't have a FAC."

Major George had done his best, but the promised air support hadn't shown.

Thuan nodded again.

Holmes knew at last that out of the events of the night he and the Vietnamese had become a team. Then in a flash it hit the newcomer that he was indeed enmeshed in a game of snares for the unwary; for the second time that morning he had been in too much of a hurry and was overlooking the obvious.

He said to Thuan: "Let's work over that first hill with the four point two mortars."

There were three tubes in the base camp. The top of the hill was still shrouded in a pale curtain of fog. But as the sun broke through and even before the mortars opened fire Holmes could see "ten to twenty VC just milling around in the open." Or were they collecting weapons? The question came aimlessly into his head and he let it evaporate there.

As the first salvo exploded—and the rounds were a little short—Holmes could see the figures vanish into the trenches atop the hill. They fired twenty or more rounds, with what results there was no way of knowing. Nothing stirred in the target area.

By 0815, the FAC had still not shown.

Holmes said: "We'd better launch the attack now or we'll miss them."

Thuan nodded agreement.

The two light companies, one marching the paddies, the other going by road, went forth while the 4.2's continued to pound away. Within approximately thirty minutes, and almost coincidentally, both companies had closed on the base of the two hills and started upward.

It was another error. They were beaten back hard. The Charlies leaned over the parapets and swept the assault lines with automatic fire as they tried to claw their way up the slope. Holmes could see the Charlies plainly. He knew before it happened that repulse was inevitable.

He said to Thuan: "We must call off the attack." Another thirty minutes was lost before the withdrawal from the high ground was completed. By then the company attacking the northern hill had lost five dead and eight wounded; the southern attack cost four KIA and eight WIA.

From atop the southern hill came the enemy's derisive yells: "Keep coming, Americans! We got you! We show you real fight!"

Holmes wondered at it. Only the Vietnamese were taking a beating. American participation was as yet a very small thing. Were the NVA misinformed or simply anxious to impress the Montagnards with their contempt for Special Forces?

At La Hai, four kilometers beyond the northern hill, there were based four Regional Force companies, advised by one Special Force lieutenant and five SF NCO's. Though administratively they were under MACV, Holmes reckoned they might be willing to help.

He called La Hai to ask: "Would you put two companies on the road and try to regain the northern hill?"

The answer was a cheerful: "Will do!"

At 0920, just as the La Hai companies started south, the FAC ship appeared overhead. Under the FAC's control were fourteen A-1E's, which was plenty. Within the next five minutes they had begun to napalm and bomb the southern hill.

There followed a slaughter grim and great, interrupted only by the FAC's first message to Holmes: "I'm being shot at and how! I can count between fifty and sixty Charlies directly under me on the hill."

Holmes said: "Man, you take it easy."

There came back only a "Roger" and a chuckle.

Fascinated by the spectacle, Holmes for those few minutes simply played spectator. As the bombs fell, he could see bodies blown high in the air from out of the trenches to fall heavily on the slope. But even as these dead were lofted, other enemy soldiers jumped from the trenches to reach for the corpses as they struck earth and drag them away.

Directly above Holmes (he was at the base of the hill) one

rifleman reared up from the trench, his weapon pointed straight toward the American, at forty-meter range. Holmes in that split second thought he was a goner. Suddenly the figure of the rifleman dissolved in a pillar of fire. A napalm container had exploded next to him. By the time Holmes saw the human torch and sensed what had happened, another Charlie had lassoed the figure and was pulling it to cover along the trench line.

Sergeant Tucker yelled: "God Almighty, I have never seen anything like that."

Then in a low tone, Tucker added: "They've got to be NVA."

Holmes, who had been no less startled by the spectacle, said quietly: "I don't know. I can't tell you a thing. This is my first time."

The sensation of shock was such that he felt he wanted to upchuck but couldn't quite make it. Tucker's excitement and Holmes's must have been of quite a different order.

At 1045 Holmes and Thuan decided that there had been enough of the air strike. The troops moved up to the high ground without further trouble.

Rarely has such a move in battle been so utterly anticlimactic.

There was not one brayed or burned body on the hilltop and not a single weapon. The enemy had gone as quickly as a light blown out. The place looked as dead as a VC graveyard.

The trenches were hardly immaculate, but there were no real blood trails, though freshly turned-over earth, with some traces of scarlet here and there, showed where the trails had been scruffed out.

Holmes rubbed his eyes in disbelief. It had been magic, like a Blackstone trick done in a moment before one's eyes. He had seen men killed, yet where he looked there were no dead.

A few feet lower down than the military crest of the reverse slope, Thuan and his people came across six Civilian Irregular Defense Group bodies and a few shattered American weapons. And what had been left of these forlorn friendlys from the battered company out of Dong Tre was about all they found that really mattered.

The fighter bombers that had been overhead chased the fleeing NVA all the way along the narrow valley leading northeastward from the scene of the fight. The FAC called back to Holmes over the radio: "We are receiving heavy fire from positions along the main trail. I can't quite make it out."

But the FAC and his flock of ships were by this time in heavy embarrassment. They had expended too much of their fighting loads in the attack against the hill. At the ground control position, Holmes felt furious about the minor perversities of life. Opportunity yawned and there was no one to move in. The Americans aloft could look but they couldn't shoot.

Holmes felt still worse a few minutes later when another message came from the FAC: "I am over a village. Don't know its name. [This was the place called Trung Luong.] I can see at least one battalion in movement toward it and getting very close. They act like they want to be seen. They are waving at us. But we can't do anything about it."

Here was the one moment at the opening of a large battle solemn and significant above all others. But there was no one at hand to read the warning that the NVA had chosen a battlefield prepared to their advantage and were baiting the ground.

Holmes was simply puzzled by the mystery.

Only a captain, green at the game, as smart as he was eager, Holmes was learning fast, though not quite fast enough. He pondered the riddle for a few minutes, then dropped it, there being other things to do. That bit of priceless information was not passed along to higher commands, and as to conclusions, Holmes had none.

There was another Holmes, first name Sherlock, who might have missed the main point, also. And the two intelligence sergeants made Holmes none the wiser.

At 1130, Thuan, under prodding by Holmes, sent one CIDG

platoon northeastward to prowl the trail leading toward Trung Luong. To put it mildly, the platoon was in no rush to get ambushed. In the style of Ferdinand the Bull, it picked the sweet June flowers and otherwise dawdled. Perhaps security was better served that way.

Almost two hours later, a message came to Thuan from the platoon's RTO that ran as follows: "We have come across eighteen freshly dug graves along the trail."

Holmes said to Thuan: "They better stop and dig into them."

Thuan shrugged, but did his best to make it a direct order.

After the first grave was opened, Thuan knew it was useless to press the point further.

His troops had uncovered an enemy body clad in khaki, the hands still clutching a new AK-47 rifle in prime condition. That done, the CIDG soldiers dug in their heels and refused to touch another grave. Autopsies were not their business. Their superstitions had much too low a threshold. The balk stood, and in that way most of the afternoon was lost.

Thuan said: "They think bad luck if they open more graves."

Holmes nodded, which was as close as he ever came to ceremony, and walked away.

His mind was pondering the question: "Why would the NVA stop in flight to dig graves?"

Something stirred in his subconscious and at last a great light dawned.

The day before, Tucker had told him about an agent bringing in a report that North Vietnamese troops in the vicinity were constructing coffins and that soldiers from an NVA transportation battalion were digging pits that looked like graves.

Here was a first warning that had not been taken seriously. The entire scenario had been pre-planned. The graves, pre-dug along the line of retreat, were ready even before one body awaited burial.

During high noon, Holmes and Thuan had gotten together

with one of the companies that had come from La Hai, having discreetly skirted the northern hill to speed on toward Dong Tre. These CIDG soldiers were very skittish. Sensing the foot-dragging, Holmes put them under his XO, Lieutenant Peter le Clair, a Californian, who was seconded by Sergeant Bill van Meter, another Green Beret.

They moved on against the second hill. At its base the troopers stopped. Some rifle bullets whistled past their ears, none of the fire coming in bursts and all of it most inaccurate. Van Meter became disgusted at the lack of movement and stormed the hill alone. The one-man charge was all it took to settle matters. There was no one atop the hill to turn Van Meter back.

Major George arrived in a Huey about 1330. Leading a handful of Thuan's irregulars, he climbed the third hill without a shot being fired. No bodies or weapons were found on the slopes. By mid-afternoon the troops from Dong Tre were once more sitting on the real estate with which they had started.

Of the eighty-two men in the company who had been posted on the three hills when the NVA attack began, twenty-six had to be marked killed in action, and seven were so badly wounded that they later died. The first missing-in-action count was fifty-one but this later dwindled to twelve as the stragglers returned day after day.

The vital statistics were the least wretched part of the story. The company had goofed miserably. It was impossible to identify one soldier who had performed creditably.

By means of a grilling interrogation, it was learned that at least one full hour before the NVA assaulted the three hills, two of the company's ambush patrols had observed "large bodies of troops" crossing the Song (River) Tra Buon. This observation was never reported. One squad leader had been charged to fire a red flare as a signal to the base camp that an enemy force had been sighted. He was so terrified that he could not obey the order. Dropping his flares and weapon, he bugged out on the run for

Dong Tre. Yet, even he, relatively speaking and within his lights, was a duty-doer and a gentleman.

Late that afternoon the company commander of the outpost force turned himself in at Dong Tre, wrapped in a yellow bedsheet but otherwise naked.

Within a few minutes thereafter, the ARVN Special Force adviser, a sergeant attached to the outpost company, arrived at the Dong Tre gate, clad like Adam except that he wore a large banana leaf over the family jewels. He looked done in.

It turned out that these two characters had been frolicking with two babes in a shack not far from the base of the first hill when the NVA attack hit against the trench line above them. They believed in making love, not war. Together they had fled the fight and the dolls at one and the same time, not tarrying to say good night or thanks. The officer, being the hardier spirit, tarried long enough to grab the bedsheet.

The adventure and its aftermath wholly broke the Vietnamese NCO. He moped about the camp for a few days, then went completely off his rocker. The lieutenant, being less brittle, ultimately fled Dong Tre and his tormenters.

A patrol was sent out to search for the hut. The dolls had fled the neighborhood. The shack was empty. The lieutenant confessed that the girls were strangers who had moved in only two nights before.

Holmes could only shake his head and wonder. Was the seduction but one more act written into the enemy scenario? Probably, very probably.

Other questions arise that may be answered without guessing. The Fight of the Three Hills was but a warm-up for the big battle of Trung Luong—Operation Nathan Hale—that swiftly developed from it. In the course of a larger battle an NVA lieutenant was captured and he talked freely.

It was his battalion, the Seventh Battalion of the 18th NVA Regiment, that had attacked the three hills. The battalion's main object was to destroy the Dong Tre garrison. The Eighth Battalion of that same regiment had been waiting in ambush along the road running from the base to the three hills. Its task was to slaughter the reaction columns.

Directly to the south of Dong Tre, almost within practical range of a rifle grenade, is a large camelback hill. The crest of this most imposing feature of the landscape is antenna-adorned, the hill being the nodal of camp communications.

Behind the camelback, the 85th Main Force (VC) Battalion had been waiting. When the columns moved north and the ambushing began, the 85th was to advance over the saddle of the hill and capture the base camp. The chance never came. Thuan had been right all along. By bucking both George and Holmes, the Vietnamese had saved both his soldiers and the redoubt, and what might have been a disaster was limited to a bad-enough wound.

The captured NVA lieutenant had himself led the attack on the south hill. His company, with two attached sapper squads, had crawled belly-down all the way to the trench line without being detected. The CIDG soldiers had fallen asleep in their hammocks, due to the dereliction of the two leaders who were absent, awake, and frolicking in the hay. When the sappers threw their satchel charges into the works atop the hill, that was the signal for the general attack to begin.

Except for a five-minute fight on the northern hill, the Seventh Battalion met no resistance anywhere. The capture of the three hills was completed at a cost of four soldiers lightly wounded. The green star clusters Holmes had noted were the signal that the hills were all solidly in NVA hands. By then the battalion had been ordered to stay on as a delaying and blocking force, and the U.S. air attack, after daylight came, cost it seventy killed and thirty-five wounded.

These things Holmes learned later, though he had seen enough that day to feel fairly certain that the enemy maneuvering around

Dong Tre was only a come-on, an enticement linked to some much larger and more devious design. His was not hunch thinking; the facts, when added, led to no other conclusion.

Still, Holmes did not send along these vivid impressions to the nearby United States commands. Making an intelligence analysis was not exactly his business, and besides, he was much too new on the job. He scarcely knew which nearby commands were interested in happenings at Dong Tre.

Nor did anyone at First Cavalry Division (Airmobile) or from the paratroop headquarters in Tuy Hoa, come posting to Dong Tre to ask Holmes: "Will you now tell us everything you know, and include anything you suppose?"

And that was the hell of it.

Holmes was perfectly ready to talk. But a newly arrived captain is rarely regarded as a possible fount of wisdom by his superiors who have been long in the territory.

So warnings went unspoken and hard charging spared no time to caution. Of this came much that should not happen to a dog.

It never occurred to Captain Holmes that he had performed very creditably through this, his first real trial at arms. He was a little chagrined that Thuan had outguessed him as to what the enemy had in mind for Dong Tre and he thought, somewhat vaguely, that he was overlooking some detail of major importance. He continued to puzzle over it.

THE VIEW FROM
THE HIGH LEVEL

CHASING THE Cong or the NVA is much like going after the Irishman's flea, as Major General Jack Norton learned once again in the course of the battle that opened with the attack on Dong Tre.

In the beginning, there seemed little chance that the incident at the Special Forces base would finally drag in the cavalry. A battalion of the 327th Infantry (First Brigade, 101st), based on Tuy Hoa, was the designated I Force Victor (II Corps) reaction element for the area, and Trung Luong Valley was only a short chopper hop from the port city, while the armed perimeter of the First Cavalry Division near An Khe was almost one hour distant.

Moreover, the Division was fully occupied, and like its commander, most of its fighting troops were far off in the western Central Highlands. The Division had just come through a hard go in the Crazy Horse operation that had ended on 5 June. (The story of that operation is told in my book, *Battles in the Monsoon*.)

Its Second Brigade was beating about the Ia Drang Valley in an operation tabbed Hooker I, which yielded the troops almost no chance for meaningful shooting practice, though it gave them plenty of time to go bathing in the rock-bound and crystal-clear pools of the cascading Ia Drang.

On 15 June, the First Brigade, under Colonel Jack Hennessey, was bucketed west from An Khe to make an air assault on the Buon Blech mountain area out of Pleiku. The First Battalion of the Eighth Cavalry, with artillery and air support elements, under the command of Lieutenant Colonel Barney Broughton, was standing by as the Corps reaction force in that area.

Norton went that way because most of his troops were disposed along the western plateau. He also had high hopes that Hooker I, to be followed up by Hooker II, would bag some part of the NVA's 18-B Regiment, reported concentrating somewhere in the mountain mass that Hennessey's people were working over. Almost needless to say, these operations did not get their names from the two hookers of Dong Tre.

In late afternoon of 18 June, Norton, then at Pleiku, got the news that the Green Berets and their CIDG charges at Dong Tre had become "heavily engaged by enemy forces of unknown size."

He felt only mildly interested. His thoughts were on Hookers I and II and the prospect of smiting 18-B Regiment somewhere in the mountains. What he didn't know—the information that might have brought him out of his chair—was that it was the 18-B Regiment that was putting on a trap-setting performance in the Trung Luong Valley, eighty kilometers to the east.

No one else on the friendly side being for the present one whit wiser than Norton about where the flea was really hopping, Hennessey's wild goose chase had to continue for several more days along with Norton's excessive expectations. The thought of it is more than enough to make a good soldier turn pink.

On 19 June, Norton talked by radio to Colonel George Becker, one of his ADC's, and to Colonel Hal Moore, commanding the Cav's Third Brigade. Moore, who has an uncanny instinct for smelling out a good fight coupled with an inability to leave it alone, was panting for a quick move to Dong Tre.

Norton, not yet ready to give up on the two Hookers and unwilling to strip An Khe of minimum security forces (two battalions), authorized Becker and Moore to hop over to Tuy Hoa and have a good look.

Norton told them: "If it's a big enemy, we'll be prepared to take over."

Such it proved to be, though the Cav began edging into the act before the signs read conclusively that, far from being a small sideshow, the situation was a three-ring circus.

Not only was the still-to-be-identified 18-B Regiment massing, maneuvering, and mooching in the Trung Luong Valley, but so were the NVA 32nd and 66th Regiments, or at least their major elements.

These were old enemies, components of the same Division that the cavalry had engaged in the far western highlands in December 1965 and the following February. In March and again in April, the First Brigade had been lifted to the Chu Pong Mountains along the Cambodian border and there fought the Eighth Battalion of 18-B Regiment and the Eighth Battalion of the 66th.

It was mighty unkind of 18-B and the 66th and a mean trick to play. Hennessey and people were wearing out their jungle boots to no good end, threshing out the unpeopled Buon Blech range. Norton was crossing his fingers and talking up the possibility that the better part of three regiments might be zapped and bagged in Hooker II—and all the time the little stinkers had sideslipped him by the distance that an NVA soldier can conquer in approximately one week.

The only lesson in all of this is that when intelligence is 180 degrees off, boundless mobility makes for great wastes of energy as well as leaping when there has been no looking.

Had Holmes been flown at once to talk things out with the G2 at An Khe or the battalion commander, Lieutenant Colonel Joseph Wasco, Jr., at Tuy Hoa or Jack Norton in Pleiku, he could have said that which might have availed a sounder approach to operations. Major General Swede Larsen at Corps HQ might also have read more correctly the unfolding big picture.

But things are seldom done that way in our Army. The reason why they are not too often passes understanding.

INTO THE
VALLEY

THE PITCH HAD already been made from Corps HQ in Nha Trang for a reaction force to get going well before Captain Holmes finished beating out the high ground around Dong Tre.

In mid-afternoon of 18 June orders reached the two companies of Second Battalion, 327th Regiment, that were on standby just outside Tuy Hoa. They were to assault as quickly as possible into the Trung Luong Valley. The battalion's Bravo Company was at the extreme western end of the Central Highlands garrisoning the outpost at Dak To, though it would soon be winging eastward.

The bad news arrived just in time to make Lieutenant Richard W. Whelan feel jaundiced though he hadn't a touch of malaria. A twenty-eight-year-old citizen of Clear Lake, Iowa, and a graduate of Iowa University, Whelan had been in Vietnam just twenty-four hours, and here he was already being launched into a war of which he knew little, as acting XO of a rifle company of which he knew less. It was enough to give any soldier the willies.

Charley Company prepped at Tuy Hoa through the night, and at 1100 next morning mounted up and rode, landing at high noon on a cold LZ of such little subsequent use that it went nameless. A reticulation of hard-baked, unworked rice paddies, set amid thirty or more deserted huts and farmers' sheds, the LZ was expansive enough so that the twenty slicks carrying the outfit and its supply could all set down at one time. Such portals are rare in Vietnam.

The company formed a perimeter on the southern edge of the valley. From where the men squatted, the view was anything but formidable. No life stirred anywhere. The Trung Luong Valley, for its mile and more of width, runs evenly, a gently rising and almost treeless plain, looking more like a piece of Wyoming than anything in Southeast Asia. The ridges to the north, rising to two hundred meters or more, are without forest or noteworthy features except for patches of elephant grass and ledges of rimrock.

Running parallel to the valley, a grenade's throw from where the troops rested momentarily, was the river, a stream of creek-like proportions that had cut a trench with sheer banks rising five to eight feet above the water. That straight line of the river slashed directly across their front was the only ribbon of greenery within sight. Elsewhere the earth was tawny and the grass withered. Only the tall bamboos, rushes, and lilies that bordered the river looked inviting and troops felt an urge to go there, if only to cool off.

The gently rising plain beyond was without blemish, with not a military position to be seen. About five hundred meters north of the river a dirt road ran parallel to it, entering a group of hamlets somewhat more than a mile to the northeast. This was the object on which Charley Company was targeting. At least a battalion had been reported by the air observers as making a big play at Trung Luong village, and Charley Company was going after it—a single company.

First Platoon led off, moving in an inverted "V" formation to-ward the river, there to turn right and continue eastward, walking the stream bed. Weapons Platoon moved off at a slant across the open ground south of the river, to join First Platoon at the point where the river came even with the hamlets.

It didn't work.

There were trails, dilapidated plantations, and scrubby vegetation south of the river, and in wending its way east, Weapons Platoon strayed off.

At 1245, First Platoon's column started out of the riverbed to go for Trung Luong on its own, and within less than a minute came under intense machine-gun and AK-47 fire. Until then, there was not a single sign of danger, and no sound but the distant barking of dogs. The fire came from across the rice paddies, and was seemingly based along the bottom of a small knoll lying south of the nearest hamlet.

The platoon commander, Lieutenant Charles Beagle of Memphis, Tennessee, had led the assault, after checking with and getting authority from Lieutenant Luther Woods, the company commander. Woods had stayed behind with the main body of the company.

Beagle had done the right thing, and it had worked out in exactly the wrong way. Instead of committing the whole platoon to the riverbed, where it would have been hidden by the banks but would also have been blind to anything that came against it, Beagle had peeled off one fire team from each two squads to walk along the top of the bank.

So the movement had become a giveaway, under observation all the time. The bank walkers were the men who were cut down. And at the same time, an enemy patrol trying to cross the river from the south got away with a sneak approach and hit the platoon from the rear, which put the Americans in a cross fire.

The red harvest was eight men down and wounded, quicker than one might say Jack Robinson. Among the casualties was

Lieutenant Daniel Larned, a faithful gunner FO who took a bullet in his right shoulder; and the heavy jolt as he caught the slug spun him backward into wind-gone collapse. Such was the turning point.

At thirty-eight, with eighteen years in the Regular Army, Platoon Sergeant James D. Arnold of Spartanburg, South Carolina, is an oldster by American standards. Until that moment he had been going along with what the folks up top had ordered.

Arnold now spoke his piece: "I think we better get the hell out of here; we are hunting tigers with popguns."

Beagle could not but agree.

Here was one of the wisest suggestions made during the whole affair, and something is to be said for a Beagle with such high intelligence.

They backed off, re-treaded the stream bed, this time with no scouts out.

After First Platoon got back to the company, it shifted position a little to the eastward, coming to rest next to an elevated piece of ground abutting on the river. It was a terrain that looked as if an American housing development authority had begun to work it over.

The time was about 1400.

First Sergeant Kenneth R. Peplow, forty-four, of Clarksville, Tennessee, with twenty-two years as a professional soldier, was the oldest EM in the operation, though at this juncture he knew scarcely more about it than the youngest. Out of the ARVN he had gleaned the wisp of information that "enemy troops are moving somewhere in the vicinity, their numbers unknown," which might have been said of any number of places in Vietnam in the same hour. Next he got the information that "Wild Gypsy" (Wasco's code name) was to move in and see what could be done about it. So the old soldier, Peplow, was somewhat browned off. He had been groping about for too many hours and was tiring of banks festooned with tightly planted bamboo that screened out the horizon as effectively as the walls of a fort.

At the same time the experience was like being in an antbed freshly stirred. All hands were moving about, though the outfit had gone into perimeter chiefly to evacuate a few casualties and avert a few more. The defensive perimeter looped north across the river, which was a beautiful stream of swift running water nonetheless unaccountably milky. In that direction, the defended ground reached halfway to the road, while at the same time southward of the creek it enclosed the snubbed-off hill that some of the soldiers called a sugarloaf and others termed a tabletop.

It was, in fact, neither, but rather a partly man-made monstrosity, an elevation of dirt with almost sheer embankments, also of soft earth. Its flat top averaged about twelve meters of height above the surrounding flat terrain.

The surface of the hill, which was about a hundred feet wide where it fronted on the river, and four hundred feet from end to end, was almost exactly level. It had been planted in sorghum, and the stubble of a last crop still speckled the surface. The whole mound consisted of loose dirt. Some particularly industrious Viet farmer must have spent years cutting away at the dome to get a workable field out of the eminence.

Lieutenant Whelan was no better satisfied with the way things were going than was Peplow.

Dreaming up something better to do was the real problem.

Fire was still coming against the sugarloaf from the ridges to the north, or from somewhere between the hill and Trung Luong village to the northeast. Its source remained baffling. Such was its relative accuracy, however, that little freedom of movement remained.

While the men waited for the dust-off Huey to pick up earlier casualties PFC Don Cook was killed by a bullet through his

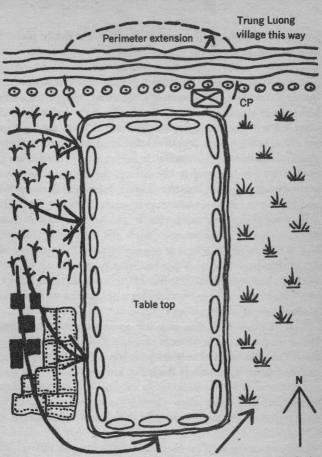

Trung Luong village this way

Perimeter extension

CP

Table top

N

The NVA charge on C/2/327. The area to the east of the Table top, a planted field, became the LZ later. The symbols follow:

Bamboo screen

Dried rice paddies

Banana grove

Foxhole line

temple. The death was the more chilling because the hit seemed to be an outright fluke.

So another Huey had to be called in while Whelan tried to take the measure of his problem. He reckoned that the VC weapons were being worked over a 350-meter front and that the nearest fire points must be all of 300 meters distant. (There is no check on the accuracy of this calculation.) On the basis of hunch more than reckoning, he called on Bravo Battery, 320th Artillery, based on the crossroads eastward of Trung Luong, to shell the ground between the road and the ridges to the north.

Lieutenant Larned, the FO, having been laid low by his shoulder wound, Whelan took over the corrections and gradually walked the fires north and up the ridge slopes. A flight of four F-4C's happened to come over just as the artillery slacked off, and Whelan sent them against the high ground on an east-west run with napalm and small bombs. From the time Cook was hit until the heavy weapons had done their work the span was no more than twenty minutes. Yet the more distant enemy fires seemed to taper off thereafter.

That impression of tapering off could have been illusion, however, caused by mounting pressure at much closer range. Enemy parties were now working against the perimeter from east and west by crawling along the line of bamboo that curtained the stream. Whelan's people were under the intense glare of the sun. The VC snipers wiggled along the grassy bank in deep shade on the far side of the bamboo. It was impossible to see movement.

The recourse was to go to ground in the foxholes that ran all the way around the crown of the sugarloaf. They were old pits, dug by the VC. It was an unsatisfactory solution, but it was better than getting men killed for no good purpose.

Even less satisfactory was what happened to PFC Joe Kinikin, of Seaside, California. He had just returned from being hospitalized for a pongi stake wound and the jungle boots he wore had far too much mileage on them. Striding through the deep grass at the base of the sugarloaf, he dropped into a pit; the pongi stake, poisoned, tore through the ball of his foot. This time he went to hospital for forty-three days. He made only one comment: "Hell, here I go again."

When Battalion Commander Wasco flew into the position at 1600, he brought with him the mortar platoon and the antitank platoon by way of reinforcements. That raised Charley Company to a strength of 140. To their disgust, these newly arrived special elements were told to forget their heavy weapons and were fed into the perimeter as riflemen. This was the idea of Wasco, who was trying to stretch a truncated battalion farther than is possible even with an overstrength one.

Wasco is a commander who uses words as sparingly as if they were officially rationed. Still, he has a delightful grin when he chooses to use it, and as a tactician he is nobody's fool. Wasco never speaks without thinking, but so pronounced is his professional reserve that a stranger must wonder whether he can distinguish between minimum voice contact and control.

Wasco said what he had to say to Woods and Whelan and flew back to Tuy Hoa. There really wasn't very much that could be said, since the problem remained inscrutable, and another day had been lost with nothing gained. Whelan was beginning to think that combat was mainly another word game, like Scrabble.

Charley Company spent that night in perimeter without sweat and little more sleep. The foxholes on the sugarloaf were deep enough; the night was warm, the sky cloudless. But the men's rest was harassed by too many rifle grenades exploding amid the sorghum stubble and too many snipers sneaking along the bamboo curtain to gasconade with a few rounds of fire and then skedaddle. The name of the game was to make yourself as large a nuisance as possible.

Whelan had some of his soldiers stack brush along the paddy banks that lay north of the river and within the perimeter. The tinder would be lighted with trip flares should the enemy stage a night attack. Some dousing with gasoline was done. This was Whelan's first creation, or tactical adaptation of things he had read about like the fougasse, and he felt extremely proud of it. Two listening posts were put north of the river about twenty meters out from the perimeter line, which is too short a distance within which to locate LP's. Both were well camouflaged, however, and were provided with overhead cover in ground about a hundred meters north of the river trench. One wonders why troops were given all of this hard labor. The natural line of defense was the river itself, as any Benning graduate should have been able to see.

The antitank platoon, under Staff Sergeant Charles F. Proctor, twenty-one, of Atlanta, Georgia, was placed north of the river.

Proctor wasn't aching for trouble, but he couldn't sleep. Around 2100, glancing southward, he saw a VC, or what he thought was a Charlie, standing in clear silhouette on the north end of the "tabletop." An artillery flare, just fired, so placed him. Being reasonably sure of his target, Proctor fired with a machine gun, at a range of fifty or so meters, and killed the intruder, without even stirring the garrison, a fact which surprised Proctor.

Emboldened by success, he put out a patrol to flush the ground to the east, between himself and the hamlets. The patrol at once collided with an enemy patrol bumper-to-bumper. Both parties, hardly farther apart than pool-table length, heaved grenades. One enemy grenade exploded directly against the body of Spec 4 Wayne Nelson and killed him, so ending his first day ever under fire.

Proctor thought that his own men had drawn more blood; later he described how his men had bombed right together, and how at least four grenades had exploded right among the Charlies, and how, after that he saw "four of them walk away as if they were carrying two others." According to Proctor, at least two of the enemy were blowing police whistles as they moved off, not the least bizarre touch to his story. The Americans followed the enemy for a distance, firing their M-16's to no worthwhile purpose. This somewhat forlorn enterprise mystified Proctor as much as anyone who heard of it.

The CP's were all north of the river on a flat sand bed. There was one LP up river, perched on the bank of the stream and another down river, lodged in a bend thereof. These were not sound dispositions, since the strong ground lay south of the river, and the company was too far spread. Still, the enemy did not come on that night when this small force was so heavily disadvantaged.

Why not?

There is no answer.

But the flare ship, Smokey the Bear, was overhead much of the night illuminating the valley, and possibly the flares provided the deterrent.

The Americans attacked again, over the sâme line, at 0900 next morning. Alpha Company, under Captain Furgeson, was still at Tuy Hoa and about to receive its orders. High command was still obviously underestimating NVA strength in the valley; the hamlets at Trung Luong had been little worked over by heavy weapons.

First Platoon led off, moving in two columns with both columns staggered, every other man being five paces to the flank of the file ahead, the purpose being to keep casualties down if the ground happened to be mined.

Second Platoon followed along, using the same formation. It was about a hundred meters behind First.

As the two platoons left the riverbed, they moved across a grassed-over flat, followed by a gradual upgrade rather heavily boulder-strewn. Soon they were beating their way through low brush. Ahead lay a line of stunted trees from whence the previous day's fire had come. The brush was too sparse to afford effective cover, but it was better than nothing at all, and to westward lay only a barren plain. From the river to the tree line the distance was approximately three hundred meters.

For two-thirds of the way, they marched uneventfully, getting not a sign nor sound of enemy presence.

Arnold began to think that the Communists had decamped, not just from the positions held earlier, but from Trung Luong Valley. Amongst infantrymen such an idea is a common if comforting illusion.

As the men of First Platoon closed to within fifty meters of the trees, fire came at them, at first only rifles volleying, the familiar crack of the AK-47.

In the forefront, Beagle's men flattened out.

Second Platoon was given time to get its men up even and on line while the NVA fire still went high.

Within one minute the men of the two platoons were all prone and most of them were firing. Belly-down in the brush, they could see very little of one another.

Lieutenant Dee McKern, of Rice, Washington, had deployed Second Platoon to the right of First. Now he suddenly saw what he had missed all along, that his men had become committed at the hub of radial paths cut through the brush, fire lanes put there to give the enemy weapons a clear sighting.

The sad truth dawned on him when the machine gun opened fire. The gun, however, while zeroed in on one of the lanes, was getting at them from the right rear, which doubled the embarrassment.

Either the Charlies had been set to box them in when the platoons came out of the river trench or the gun had been swiftly moved to the rear position unobserved. Anyway, it was damnation.

Sergeant Richard Coughlin was hit by two machine-gun bullets through his midsection. He called out: "Medic! Medic!"

The aid man, Spec 4 Jimmy Eastham, answered: "I'm coming," though he had taken rifle bullets in both legs.

Eastham crawled to Coughlin.

As he made it, and got out some bandages, a bullet swarm caught Eastham in the head and neck and he died instantly.

The undeviating faithfulness of the United States aid man to his duty is a phenomenon beyond explanation.

Sergeant Arnold was up and yelling: "Don't fire to the right! Those are our friends!" Some of First Platoon's riflemen had missed the forward rush of Second Platoon and were turning their weapons in the wrong direction.

In Arnold's Platoon, PFC George McIlwee, of Gore, Georgia, was drilled through the chest by an SKS carbine bullet, a wound from which he died within the hour.

Between the two platoons there were seven lesser casualties, a relatively light loss that is a measure only of NVA ineptitude at shooting.

All of the bad news was getting back to Lieutenant Woods at the perimeter and it hit hard enough to make him call off the show.

Over the RT he ordered Beagle and McKern to withdraw the platoons as best they could. Whelan, the new boy acting as XO, was also using his head. He called the artillery at the crossroads, gave the coordinates, and said: "Let them have a covering smoke and plenty of it."

Beagle, McKern, and their men crawled off obliquely rearward via the left flank, taking the shortest line to the perimeter and thereby thwarting the machine gun on their right rear and any ambush pary that might have been lying in wait. With the aid of a perfectly laid-on smokescreen, they made it back to Woods, as Arnold put it, "mighty fine good."

Whelan had been sent out with Mortar Platoon well to the north of the river to provide a flanking fire that might help cover the withdrawal. He lined his men up behind the stout bank of a dry rice paddy and told them to have at it. From the position, he gave corrections to the artillery, and followed up the smoke by ordering a stonk of killing shell against the enemy-held tree line, which might better have been done in the first place. By the time First and Second Platoons had come to rest in the base next the river, Whelan's position was under fire from a reinforced NVA squad that had slipped up on his rear.

It was time to back away.

The squads were leapfrogged to the river line, though the platoon did not make it unscathed.

Whelan took a bullet in his leg and PFC Joe Thigpen was creased by a slug in the right shoulder.

By 1000, all save one were present and together. When Woods learned that Eastham's body still lay south of Trung Luong village, he blazed. He said to McKern: "Turn that platoon around, take your men back, and bring the body out." This time they went with full artillery cover, as should have been done earlier. Aided by a smokescreen and several concentrations of HE, they made the extraction and the round trip unhurt.

By then Whelan was regulating repeated strikes by gunships and the rocket artillery of the First Cavalry Division against Trung Luong village. None had been called for in the early morning, which is a pity.

On the sugarloaf men dozed or worked over their weapons through the early afternoon.

At 1400, Spec 5 Bruce Johnson, one of the company's cleaner types hailing from Duluth, was washing and shaving on a sandbar next to the river and directly in front of the sugarloaf.

Johnson was wearing only his jungle boots and his shorts. He had left his gear and weapons beside his foxhole, which in enemy country is a bit careless of an infantryman. Just one of many who were taking too much for granted, Johnson thought that the river trench on either side of him was properly outposted. So without one sobering thought he whacked away at his whiskers.

His pleasing communion with self ended when in one corner of the metal mirror which he had slid into a slash in a bamboo stalk, he saw, not more than twenty meters behind his back, two khaki-clad NVA soldiers walking toward him along a path that dipped down to the stream.

Johnson sprang for the bank and ran for the sugarloaf, baying: "Charlies! Charlies! Charlies!"

The NVA fired first.

The bullets missed the bouncing Johnson and whacked through the tent of the Mortar Platoon's CP.

Sergeant Ulysses William of the AT section was struck by bullets in both elbows and Spec 4 Gary Duboise, the Mortar Platoon's medic, was struck in the right leg, a not bad score for unaimed fire.

Spec 5 Ernie Johnson was scrambling for his machine gun.

A much faster soldier on the draw, PFC Frederick Koch, beat him to it, opened fire with the M-60, and cut down one of the Charlies as he tried to get away up the opposite bank. The body toppled backward and splashed heavily into the milky water.

Staff Sergeant Peter Tiroch, twenty-three, of Lynchburg, Virginia, yelled to Sergeant William Odom, a Floridian: "Let's go get the other sonofabitch."

Odom was game. The two sergeants bounded forward together—just a bit carelessly. As they got to the edge of the bank, the surviving enemy soldier was propped against the opposite bank holding an AF "survival rifle" dead on them, and the weapon was not shaking. Tiroch emptied an M-16 clip into him and Odom belted him with an M-79 round that didn't arm.

The NV soldier remained alive and conscious. Tiroch and Odom dragged him up the bank. He lay there smiling happily. They gave him water. He smiled on. They couldn't understand it. His pack was searched, and there came forth a packet of white powder. The medic looked it over and said: "Heroin, he's really loaded." Two hours later he died, the smile still on his face. Because of the smile, Odom and Tiroch gave him a decent Christian burial. That night several mortar rounds dug him up again.

Arnold was really taken by the incident. The company in previous days had several times prowled this area with never a VC contact. Now to have the VC come in pairs looking for a fight in broad daylight was a bit of a shock. It was a different kind of soldier from any Arnold had battled before, this diehard from the 18th NVA Regiment. Here was no ordinary malignant determination; the situation was outright grotesque. The difference shook Arnold.

At 1430 Woods sent First Platoon to make another recon down the river. Three hundred meters along, the point squad was fired upon. The point man, PFC Lewish Jackson of Los Angeles, got off a burst with his M-16, firing wildly, and saw a khaki-clad figure fall from a patch of bushes headfirst into the stream. It was the flukiest kind of hit.

They were all down now, most of them on their haunches and the bullets were whipping very close to their heads, with the volume building up, up, up. Most of the stuff was coming from the bushes along the bank.

Beagle sounded the conventional order: "Let's get the hell out of here." They backed out on all fours.

At 1630 McKern and his people felt out the situation to the westward, going in column via the stream bed, while using flankers on the high ground to both sides of it. So McKern understood from the start that the movement was being followed. Five hundred meters out, the flankers were forced to take cover between the banks by a machine gun that fired from the cover of several small huts. McKern couldn't get at the gun without deploying the platoon into the open, and he wanted no part of that. He backed off and asked for a gunship strike on the huts.

Most of the night was quiet, though the enemy tried a few small probes, which brought an intermittent exchange of fires, all negative. Woods had ordered a 75 per cent alert, although the men were edgy enough that there would have been little sleep in any case.

At 0530 Woods was squatting within the bamboo curtain, doing what becomes necessary when a bad diarrhea hits. Though it was still quite black, about ten minutes earlier Smokey the Bear had quit the valley and headed for home base, having run out of flares. From his squat in the bamboo, Woods suddenly emerged at a waddle, his pants down around his knees. He was shouting: "Mortars! Mortars!"

Whelan thought Woods was yelling for his own 81's to fire, and did not stir. Whelan was squatting not far away telling his medic, Spec 4 Duddy, and his RTO, PFC Fripp, what a fine job they were doing on the new foxhole they were digging just for him. Then he heard the whistle of a mortar round and so did they.

Duddy and Fripp jumped for the hole and made it, just as three mortar rounds exploded along the river bank. It was a very tight pattern. Clued in a little late, Whelan also jumped for the hole. It was a bit small.

"Somebody gotta get out of here," said Duddy.

"Or somebody will get it here," said Whelan.

The lieutenant had only a moment to enjoy his little joke. A 2.5 rocket exploded into the bamboo, one shard of which drew blood from the platoon. It had hit Whelan square in the tail. And there is no glory in such a wound for boys with a little red drum.

A second rocket blew ten meters from Arnold's foxhole. A third exploded a few feet from Staff Sergeant Pleas Byrd, a Manhattanite, whose position was fifteen meters from Arnold's.

An unidentified voice sang out: "The sarge is hit, sarge."

Arnold asked: "Where's he hit?"

The voice yelled back: "Hit right in the ass, sarge."

Arnold sent his medic, PFC Sandoval of Milbrae, California, to look Byrd over and patch him up. He had been zapped by a shard half as large as the palm of Sandoval's hand.

Came another mortar round, and this one blew Spec 4 Roy Scott right out of his foxhole and smashed him against a tree. He dropped flat, his wind gone, his right arm dangling from a compound fracture.

Before anyone could make a move to help Scott, the NVA attack came on, a charge delivered with utmost violence from the west side of the sugarloaf. Bumping the hill on that flank, and bounded on the north by the river, was a banana plantation hardly larger than a baseball diamond. The Americans had picked its fruit through the day and some had loafed in its shade. The NVA had massed there through the hours of darkness, after fording the river. That this movement went undetected is beyond sensible explanation. The NVA had waited until the preparatory mortar-rocket strike at the sugarloaf would disorganize the camp. Their strength was about that of a battalion.

It was a neatly synchronized, almost perfectly timed beginning. But Proctor, who was in charge of the defense along that side of the hill, did not go unwarned. As the last mortar round exploded atop the hill, he heard anguished screams from the banana grove. So he knew the enemy was there and would be coming on at once.

One round had missed the target hill and had fallen among the packed soldiers under the palms, hence the cries that stirred Proctor.

He yelled: "Get ready! They're going to hit us." The voice rang with a cheerfulness he did not feel. Enough men heard him so that it made quite a difference.

THE CHARGE

PROCTOR SAT NEXT to his foxhole, eyes straining to catch first sight of them. He could see nothing. The darkness was as deep as if he were passing through a tunnel.

But his ears were keen enough. He could hear cattle bellowing and bells ringing, now that the screaming had died out. And that told him much. The enemy would come on driving the cows before them to absorb the punishment. The front of the herd now sounded as if it were not more than thirty meters from the base of the hill, and in that moment Proctor heard the shrill blow of a whistle.

The word was passing from foxhole to foxhole: "They're coming on behind the cows. Give it to the cows!"

They did with rifle fire and grenades, and better than that, with mortars. They heard the cries of animals in terror, and mixed with it the screaming of men. They could still see nothing.

Now grenades were falling all along the foxhole line and cries of: "Medic! Medic!" arose out of the dark. Only from these did Proctor know that the grenades were hitting home, for he could still see nothing.

Spec 4 Melvin Elliott was the first man lost during the charge; his right leg was blown off. Proctor's machine gunner, PFC Kelly, took a bullet through the head and died instantly.

The light began to break just a little and Proctor could see a few dark forms climbing the glacis. Three were just below him, scrambling up the side of the hill, pulling at the weeds not more than ten meters away. Proctor lay flat and rolled an unpinned grenade down the slope. It exploded right among them. That is the way his men were fighting all along the line—lying flat and rolling grenades down the slope. There was no need to worry about cattle making it over the scarp, the bank was far too steep. The cattle were a shield only as far as the base of the hill and no farther.

Still, the enemy grenades continued to take a toll. PFC Robert Peach was hit by a bullet and a grenade shard in the same moment, and died. His two foxhole mates were slightly wounded by pieces of the grenade. Proctor moved with his medic, Spec 4 Porter, to take over their now undefended location, doing so in the nick of time. Four enemy soldiers were struggling up the bank just below the foxhole. Proctor grenaded and hit them fair on, while from the side PFC Myree emptied an M-16 clip into them. The two lightly wounded had gone for first aid.

PFC's Edgar Ralston and Angel Velarde were knocked out of the fight when hit in the head by rocket frags. Sergeant Condon and Spec 4 Richard Vester were killed outright. How it happened cannot be told. No one saw them die; it was too dark to follow them all the way. The scenario went something like this. Condon raised up from his foxhole, got shot with a bullet, pitched forward and rolled down the slope. Vester followed to try to save him and became lost to sight. Later their bodies were found together.

One North Vietnamese, dropped near the top of the slope, still clutched an SKS carbine with bayonet fixed. When Vester became lost in the shadow, Spec 4 Glenn Basket jumped for the carbine and rolled down the slope to go after his two comrades. From a foxhole dead ahead and about ten meters off, a Charlie fired on him with an AK-47. Basket charged right into him and gutted him with the knife on the SKS in as rare an incident as is afforded by the Vietnam war, where the bayonet is practically unused by our side.

His emotions relieved, Basket returned to the hill, not risking a search for the bodies. Then as if suddenly recollecting, he went down the slope again, and became lost to sight. In a minute or so he was back, dragging both bodies. Phenomenally, he made it halfway up the slope. Then an enemy bullet got him through the back. He fell, then got slowly to his feet as if his weight were too great for him. Another soldier jumped downslope and helped Basket to the top. Of these actions by his men Proctor caught only fleeting glimpses now that the light was breaking, and such was the pressure on him that he could neither sing praise nor marvel.

There was no way that the platoon could fight and keep itself protected. That was the forfeit exacted from it by the peculiar ground of the tabletop. Fire from enemy rifles and machine guns was sweeping from flank to flank just above the crest of the hill and all along its western face. If the men stood up to use their M-16's, they would be mowed down. If they stayed low in the foxholes, they could not see anyone coming at them up the slope. The only alternative was for all hands to lie flat on the ground, faces forward, peering over the slope. It had to be a defense with grenades, or none at all. And already the supply of grenades was running out.

Proctor was on the RT talking to Woods: "We must have grenades. Keep them coming, all you've got."

Woods didn't have to be told. Elsewhere around the perimeter, individuals had anticipated the need and were already acting. Lieutenant Allen B. Christiansen, the Mortar Platoon leader, was on the way to help Proctor; he had a squad with him. McKern was coming up with another squad. Whelan went through his platoon stripping everyone of frag grenades, then headed for the hill with three of his men helping him to carry the load.

Yet in the end it was not the timely arrival of these reinforcements that saved Proctor's thin line. There were two other factors. The chief one was the low quality of enemy fighting supply. The NVA was using potato masher grenades, and five out of six of the bombs proved to be duds. Before the fight was halfway along, the western parapet was littered with them. More of Proctor's people were hit and bruised by falling, unexploded grenades than were wounded by fragments.

The other element in saving Proctor's unit was the arrival overhead of gunships and Sky Raiders at precisely the propitious moment when the light was fulling. The gunships were fitted with M-79 launchers in their noses. The A-1E's were napalm-loaded.

The fight had been going for about forty minutes when Whelan, the green lieutenant who had become roustabout in his first go at combat, gave them their working orders. The target was to be the banana grove just west of the sugarloaf.

Even as the aircraft began turning to make their passes, Proctor could see several squads of NVA rushing forward through the banana palms to reinforce the attack against the sugarloaf. Then suddenly the squads halted and turned about. Proctor had heard a prolonged blast on a whistle.

He said: "That must be the end of it; the whistle is blowing recall."

He hastened to see if he was right.

And it was the end—except for the administrative details and tidying up. The dust-off choppers were already landing in the buckwheat field to the east of the hill which was to become the new LZ. They had been circling overhead for some minutes, Woods having put in his call early in the game.

A few snipers were still about, so troops moved gingerly to

the task of investigating what ruin had been wrought. More than an hour passed before Proctor and the others on the sugar-loaf moved out to inspect the harvest within the grove of palms.

At the base of the sugarloaf they found nine dead cows. Scattered along the slopes and within the grove they counted eighty-three NVA corpses. They also picked up eleven enemy rifles, all with bayonets fixed.

One wounded NVA lieutenant had been left behind during the withdrawal. He had regained consciousness by the time Proctor came along, so he was packed off to the aid station. He meekly submitted to treatment, but even while his wound was being dressed he swallowed poison and died.

Woods & Company were still cleaning up the place when around noontime Captain Plummer & Company, out of First Cavalry Division, arrived to reinforce the position.

Plummer's men, after a hard march that had emptied all canteens, were so athirst that they had water on the brain. Plummer's first question was: "How about your water supply?"

Woods said: "We're drinking from the river."

Plummer protested: "But there are enemy dead in that stream."

Woods said simply: "It's the best I can do for you."

Plummer looked at him as if Woods had just escaped from a zoo.

O THE WEST-
ward in the Special Forces entrenched camp at Dong Tre, Captain
Holmes could hardly believe what was happening all around him.

The greenness was wearing off faster than he had thought possible. More remarkable still, whereas three days earlier he had
felt very much alone as he and the two intelligence sergeants
pondered a problem far beyond their means, the place now
swarmed with rank, relievers, and writers.

General officers and bird colonels were hopping in and out of
Dong Tre in such numbers that Holmes knew it was time for a
mere captain to retire to a quiet corner and sit. The Cavalry
Division has taken charge.

Moreover a press camp of imposing dimension had been set up
amid the base to shelter and feed a platoon of correspondents
flown in from Saigon. Their descent on Dong Tre, which was in
such contrast to their indifference toward other battles of the
summer, was no accident.

Major Chuck Siler, the rotund and overworked PIO of the
Cavalry Division, had flown in person to the capital on a recruit-
ing mission. His sales pitch to the correspondents was about as
follows: "Colonel Hal Moore will be in command of this one.
He's good copy, you know."

Siler had discreetly refrained from using the adjective "sexy," which the press used to speak of a commander with color and dash. It took just such an approach to get the Saigon press corps off its duff.

By these signs it may be judged that Operation Nathan Hale had become the focal point of theater attention.

To recapitulate, General Larsen at II Corps HQ early on Monday, 20 June, after looking over the mounting resistance being encountered by the insufficient forces committed from the one battalion of the 327th, had decided to reinforce with Colonel Broughton's battalion (1/8th). This battalion from the First Cavalry Division was the Corps reserve.

General Jack Norton was still going along with Hooker II, the operation in the far western Central Highlands seeking the bird that by this time had flown on to create new problems just off the eastern seaboard.

Broughton's battalion was lifted that day by C-130's and flown to South Tuy Hoa where they transferred to Hueys for insertion into the battle area. With the coming of Broughton's battalion, Colonel Hal Moore had taken over.

Moore, getting a somewhat distorted picture of what he was up against, immediately began to press General Norton for more troops; as things worked out, he overbid the hand. Norton, who had not yet given up on Operation Hooker II, was shuttling back and forth daily between the western mountains and the eastern seaboard, spending much of his time in the air, piloting his command Huey. He alerted the First Battalion of the Seventh Cavalry to go next, should infantry reinforcement be needed. An artillery battery was displaced from Camp Radcliff, the Division base, to Dong Tre.

Not until 22 June was the decision made to scrub Hooker II so that the Cavalry Division might pay undivided attention to the unpleasantness in the Trung Luong Valley. Thereby a situation initially underestimated phased into overcommitment.

The Second Battalion of the Seventh, commanded by Lieutenant Colonel Bob Lytle, was ordered to mount up and ride. Still at Camp Radcliff, and much closer to the scene than most of the elements thrown into Operation Nathan Hale, the Second Battalion was nevertheless in worse condition than any other unit for sudden movement. The night before the battalion had thrown a party, something extra—a shrimp dinner: raw shrimp, cooked shrimp, and the trimmings. The shrimp was bad. By morning light the battalion was ill with food poisoning. Yet it complied with the order. The choppers flew out loaded with men heaving and retching.

Second Battalion landed by night in an unimproved field a short walk from the outer trenches of Dong Tre. The field had been smudge-pot lighted to bring in the Caribous. The illumination brought in also a circle of enemy snipers firing out of the darkness, which turkey-shooting ignored the Caribous while downing a half-dozen cavalrymen with wounds. The irregulars within the base camp suffered not at all and were no less surprised by the return of the enemy than were the takeover soldiers of Norton's Division.

The harassment ended before the troopers had time to deploy. And that was just as well. They were in no condition to fight.

Other Division elements, more than a hundred klicks farther removed from the scene than Lytle's people, had preceded them to Dong Tre. The war provides many other dramatic examples of the extraordinary mobility of the air cavalry, a concept tried and proved on numerous fields following its entry into the Vietnam fighting in the autumn of 1965. The First Cav elements could be displaced over great space to their new battlefield within a couple of hours. Via the road the movement would have taken a minimum of two days and troops would not have arrived relatively fresh.

Many minds contributed to the creation of the air cavalry, but the commander who deserves the highest credit here is General H. W. O. Kinnard. He took over an organization thrown together in an hour of emergency and shaped it into a prime battlefield force operating along wholly new lines. Kinnard, incidentally, as a youth, had been chief architect of the defenses of Bastogne in December 1944.

Bravo Company, First Battalion, Eighth Cavalry, which only a month before had had such a rough go in Operation Crazy Horse, as recorded in my *Battles in the Monsoon,* had been far off to the westward when the call came. The battalion as a whole was working out of Kontum as a component of Task Force Colt and was part of the Field Force Reserve. That explains why it got orders in advance of the Division commitment. Corps headquarters at Nha Trang pulled the string and it went.

In command of Bravo was a new captain, Gerald E. Plummer, thirty-three, of Washington, D. C., a graduate of Michigan State University. Of medium height, with a quite rotund figure, Plummer is not a man to be fitted easily into one groove. Though he lacks imagination and is inclined to be impulsive, he has what the French call *courage de tête*—the boldness to trust his own reason. In discourse he is on the cold side. The company had adored Captain Roy D. Martin who had been knocked out in the Crazy Horse fight. It was gradually getting to know Plummer, a less approachable type and an officer who labors to impress his superiors.

At 1100 on 20 June Plummer had gotten the word that the company, then just returned from the field, should be readied at once for air movement to Tuy Hoa. The C130's were already standing by at the Kontum air field to do the lifting. At 1500 Plummer and his men were already in Tuy Hoa and getting a briefing on the battle from Colonel Lewis B. Brockton.

It was all very vague and unsatisfactory from Plummer's viewpoint, and he was not wrong.

There were no maps at hand.

The company was told that it would link up with Second Battalion of the 327th out in the boonies at some time after dark. But first it would go in on LZ Axe, a "one-ship landing zone" atop Hill 258. The LZ would probably be secure, since Charley Company of the 327th would go in there several hours earlier and guard it until Plummer arrived.

Plummer and his people were annoyed, mainly because they were given no idea of how the battle was shaping up, whether any previously committed units had gone in on LZ Axe, and what the situation was there at the moment. They thought they were entitled to know whether the ground was hot or cold.

These omissions were not Brockton's fault. It was not his mistake that almost everything he had told the company was wrong. The information was not coming through. Plummer and his men were the better for not knowing that on the hill things were as black as midnight.

Captain Joseph Mack, a twenty-nine-year-old citizen of Atlanta, and his 144 men of Lieutenant Colonel Wasco's other company had been tossed into a deadfall atop the mountain. In the very hour when Plummer was getting his bland briefing, Mack and his outfit had already become immobilized by death, wounds, and the freak accidents of a landing. It was LZ Axe that got the company in the neck; more than being merely hot, the LZ sizzled.

Contrary to the word given Plummer, the LZ was not a one-ship pad. It was a ridge crown sufficiently broad and flat so that almost all the slicks carrying the company could put down together—and by a savage irony that condition had furthered the company's undoing. The company had flown in early morning from Dak To in four Caribous, the lift ships having to make two round trips. By 1300 on that day all hands were airborne in Hueys out of Tuy Hoa and pointed for the battlefield.

Far from welcoming the mission, Mack felt grim about it. He knew he was being rushed unduly and his resentment did not come solely because of the fact that his operational briefing had told him far too little. Eighty per cent of his men were green replacements who had yet to face fire for the first time. Buck sergeants were leading platoons and privates were bossing squads. None of it was good. Time was needed for a shakedown. The company simply was not primed for anything but another kick in the pants.

Mack was not the kind of skipper who impressed either his enlisted people or his junior officer as a leader—at first meeting, that is. It was habitual with him to talk to all men in the same way and same tone, irrespective of rank. He was the perfectly natural man. By the time others understood this, they were won to him.

The crown of Hill 258 had been prepped, but only with napalm, which, as things turned out, worked injury on the wrong people. The two batteries in perimeter at the crossroads below Trung Luong village (B/2/320 and A/5/30 at position 071-714) had shelled the front of the ridge but had not succeeded in working over the length of the crown. From where they sat it was a next to impossible target. A ledge of rimrock standing higher than a man encircled the crest. Such rounds as did not fall short became overs. So the gunfire was wasted.

Loose boulders and a few earth hummocks bestrewed the surface. There were also a few declivities in the otherwise even, hard rock and repellent crown. Nothing green lived there, though minutes before it had been speckled with bunched dry grass. The ridge top, measuring hardly more than two acres, was now partly ablaze and elsewhere smoldering and smoking from the napalming.

Lieutenant Louis M. McDonald, a twenty-four-year-old Texas Aggie from Dallas, rode with the forward Hueys carrying

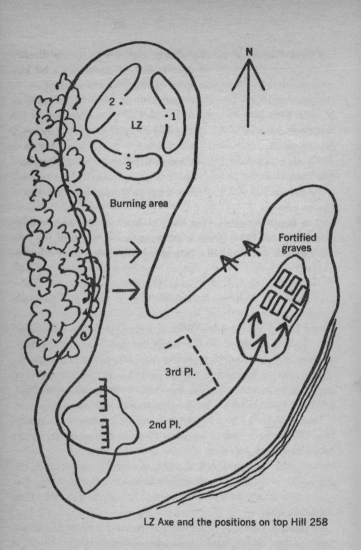

2

1

LZ

3

Burning area

Fortified graves

3rd Pl.

2nd Pl.

N

LZ Axe and the positions on top Hill 258

his First Platoon. A notably steady soldier who speaks directly to the point, he got the impression that the serial was a bit lost, because so much time was spent circling prior to landing.

Then when the lead ships put down on that heated aerie at exactly 1345, he was certain that he had been unloaded at the wrong end of the hill. Nothing had come at them as they made the approach. There was light tree cover in the other direction. With no sign of resistance close at hand, the door gunners had not even bothered to fire, which is quite unusual. It is possible they believed that the napalm drop had neutralized the top of the mountain.

The troops scrambled out and the few veterans among them stumbled outward to form a defensive circle. Some of the new men took it more casually, in trusting confidence there'd be nobody home. Then, as the first Hueys lifted and became barely airborne, while the men were scattered and upright and before the choppers were out of range, Charlie lowered the boom against the invaders.

McDonald's ship had set down so hard that the shock bounced him over the seat and onto the lap of the Huey commander, whence he slid headfirst out the panel opening and onto the ground. When he jumped up, he could see not more than six of his men. The platoon had been too widely dispersed by the landing. Wholly unaware that anything untoward was happening, McDonald started striding about to collect his people. A medic, Specialist 4 Janis, yelled at him: "Get down, lieutenant; there's fire all around."

McDonald dropped flat, his face directly behind a rock the size of a soldier's pot. In that first second or two, the rock split wide and McDonald felt a burning sensation at the side of his neck. Janis crawled over to see if he'd been hit, examined him, and said: "You're all right." McDonald took it that the hit was only imagined. Soon his blouse was dripping from the slight wound on his neck and that night he found the enemy bullet stowed in some socks in his pack.

He resumed looking for his soldiers, sliding along on his belly, but could only find a few stray hands from the Mortar Platoon. One of them, a Panamanian, was crying: "Look at me! My arm's broke. The rudder of the chopper did it."

The North Vietnamese were dug in around the southeast corner of the rimrock in platoon strength or more. An ancient graveyard near the rim had been turned into an earthwork. The positions were beautifully concealed, and though the air was blue with bullets, their source stayed a mystery. In fact, where the enemy lay and what could be done about it, Mack and his scrambled command had been given neither time nor quiet to think over. The fire at first seemed to them to come from all directions, which is ever the case when troops lie flattened and scattered under ambush. Such movement as took place in those early minutes was only that of men crawling to the nearest boulder, hummock, or depression to escape the storm of grazing fire.

Mack thought he heard at least two machine guns chattering and the crackle of a dozen or more AK-47's. But the source of the fire baffled him. The field buzzed with ricochets because of the ubiquitous boulders, which made the sounds more confusing.

Except for the wounding of one crew chief and many bullet holes, the choppers got away unhurt. Not so the company. The volley that stopped it midway in the scramble had dispersed it beyond control. Men stayed where they were, hugging protection. There were no tactics. A few of the veterans began firing. More might have done so had there been any certainty about targets.

That was about the way things went for the first thirty minutes.

Then slowly collection started here and there as a few men did things together.

Over the PRC-25, McDonald got a call from Platoon Sergeant Hargrove: "Where are you?"

When McDonald told him, Hargrove reported: "I've got most of the men here at the horseshoe-shaped end of the hill."

Mack broke in at that point: "Assemble your platoon, move to the right and flank them."

McDonald said: "The way I hear it, I don't think they lie in that direction."

Then came a cheerful note from Second Lieutenant Fred Seig, commanding Third Platoon: "I have my platoon intact; we're over the rim and I'm keeping my men very close."

Right after that call, as he moved on, McDonald bumped into the Company XO, Lieutenant George B. Pearson III, who was also scouting the source of the fire. Together they decided to collect as many M-79 thump gunners as they could find and have them concentrate fire on the tree-grown area.

By then the United States field artillery down in the valley was bracketing both forces with its fire, thereby scaring the Americans more than the Charlies who were not crawling about in the open.

Spec 4 Leon Haywood was in a cut-down squad that had deployed toward the southeast corner. These few men were the first to get a line on the enemy position. Haywood became certain of that position when a few potato masher grenades came arching toward him from out of the rocks and the gravestones. He was the only man to do anything about it. Belly-down, he crawled ten meters closer and grenaded into the rocks. But he still saw not one enemy soldier. His was the most aggressive action of the afternoon. Though the enemy position had at last become fixed by a small group, there was no way to get the word out. And with the resistance continuing and many men falling, it was impossible to re-knit the company and point it toward the object.

Well away from the beaten zone where most of the casualties were occurring, Lieutenant Seig took a bullet wound in the head. McDonald carried him to the first dust-off chopper that got away that afternoon.

Elsewhere Mack's command, at first immobilized by the fire, was becoming fully occupied in extracting its casualties and moving them to defilade on the far side of the hill, where Lieutenant Pearson supervised their evacuation.

The three stalwarts in the task of pulling back the stricken from the bullet-fire zone were the two medics, Specs 4 Janis and Philip N. Nichols, and PFC Charles McAdams, a giant Negro who had served as a cook and volunteered for rifle duty. Of the three, the chief Trojan was Nichols who pulled nine wounded men to safety while taking five bullets in his own body, which is a high price to pay for a DSC.

Then either through an enemy sneak play around the rim or a shift in direction of the fire, Seig's platoon got the buzzsaw Within less than three minutes, ten men took bullet wounds, two of them mortal. McDonald sent the word to Mack over the PRC-25. Mack had had enough. The company was wholly without water; all canteens had gone dry. His communications had gone sour. He could get through to Tuy Hoa only by relay via Dong Tre, which greatly slowed up the clearing of casualties.

Mack could only guess about the number of his casualties. But he knew there was no longer any way of beating the game. Staying on, he would only kill more good men. (The toll of the company by this time was eleven dead and twenty-seven wounded.)

Not more than one hour had passed since they had hit earth. With the grass still blazing around the crown, Mack passed out the word: "We will withdraw to the far side (northwest corner) of the rimrock." It was his intention to set up a defensive position on the far slope and call in an air strike.

The men went away crawling or belly-down, dragging off the last of the wounded and leaving behind two bodies that were prohibitively close to the enemy works. One was the body of PFC Willy Jones, later remembered by his comrades because "he had such little feet and such big boots that to do an about-face he had to get in his socks."

The hilltop began to quiet. Whether it meant that the NVA had pulled away from the southeast corner there was no way of knowing. No one ever saw them depart. Just for once, there was no higher command ship circling overhead to observe the action.

Colonel Moore, a hard charger who took his full share of risks, flew into the new position in late afternoon. He was hot and bothered. He couldn't understand why Mack had pulled back his men.

He said to the quiet man who addressed all people alike: "I want you to attack right now; there's not more than one squad holding you up."

Mack said: "Sir, I have almost fifty casualties now; I won't attack again unless supporting fires are laid on."

Moore said: "Go."

Mack replied: "Colonel, I don't give a rat's ass what you say; I am not going."

Moore dropped the argument right there and let things be as they were.

Mack had sounded both final and finished.

Moore called for a strike against the enemy side of the rim-rock, but the formation was diverted to help Furgeson in his fight against Trung Luong village.

Still without water, Mack's company stayed on the hill through the night. It finally was withdrawn at 1430 next day, counting but 47 men of the 144 who had attacked the hill. Half of the losses were heat casualties.

Plummer & Company had landed on LZ Axe at dusk of that same evening. They sat down unopposed. Before the new arrivals could talk to Mack & Company, the dark had closed.

And there were other problems. The mortars and the other

heavy bundles had been brought along sling-loaded and the Hueys had dropped them in the valley, four hundred meters wrong. Plummer called for the 105 battery in the valley to fire flares above LZ Axe so that he could get along with his tidying-up chores.

With the help of the lights, Staff Sergeant William C. Odom of Fayetteville, North Carolina, led a small party downslope and retrieved the lost bundles.

There was still no fire.

Charley Company of Barney Broughton's battalion was landed on Hill 258 to attack from the westward toward Trung Luong hamlet next day.

The night was well along when the air strikes came in, squandering spectacularly a plethora of bomb power and bullets on dead ground.

Plummer had thrown out white smoke to mark the edge of the rimrock and the plumes stood straight and silvered under the artillery flares as if in a spotlight.

The planes came in as low as possible for their passes.

The 20-mm. fire was so close to Plummer's lines that it kicked up gravel and slivers of rock, stinging the faces of men in the fire team led by Sergeant Allen Wright. Plummer knew before the show was over that he was going through nothing better than a misplaced training exercise.

The rest was anticlimax. Bravo's men arose and closed on the rocks where the NVA had nested through the afternoon. They found a dozen or so bodies. Some had been beaten up by the fires thrown against the southeast corner. But each corpse had been carefully booby-trapped by the NVA survivors and all other weapons had been removed. They had taken their time. The picture was enough to suggest that the live enemy had been gone for hours. That face of the ridge was quite barren. So they had exited like ghosts.

Moore was back on the hill soon after dawn. He told Plummer

that he wanted Bravo to link up with the 327th elements on the sugarloaf hill just as quickly as possible. Like ten years in the penitentiary, it was easy to say and hard to do.

Moore, by this time, was almost painfully aware that he was poking at a hornet's nest. No brigade commander in Vietnam had battled the VC and NVA on as many fields and none had been more successful at searching and smashing. Utterly aggressive, self-reliant, and seemingly tireless, Moore asked as much of troops as they could possibly give. They went the limit for him because they admired his dash and boldness and were ever ready to admit it.

This once, however, the view from the high ground told him nothing. It merely expanded the area of the puzzle without revealing the key to it. The shadeless ridge top already sizzled under the sun of early morning and Moore was sweating, partly from the heat of the day.

A ROMP IN
THE SUN

AMONG
Americans who are closest to the fighting in Vietnam there is never much scuttlebutt about how their piece of the war is going.

The Division or the Brigade may be in battle but very little of how it is faring filters back either to its own base camp, to fellow warriors in the next province, or even to the reaction force that stands by like a bucket brigade to rush in should the blaze get beyond control.

This dearth of information on situation that might prove useful to soldiers who may become directly concerned with the business at hand is not an oddity peculiar to Vietnam operations. The void closest to the scene is common to all war and the wonders of the era of electronics have provided little fill. Whether this void works out for better or worse, insofar as troop morale goes, no one has ever been able to establish beyond reasonable doubt. Occasionally it becomes a bane to effective action by support forces. But in the end all things seem to even out. Where ignorance is bliss, 'tis sometimes jollier not to be wise.

Such was the only possible solace for Captain Charles T. Furgeson and his soldiers of Alpha Company, First Battalion, 327th, on the morning of 19 June 1966, when the summons hit them at their base camp at Tuy Hoa. They knew only that several CIDG companies around Dong Tre had been clobbered aplenty and that they had to go. To most of them Dong Tre was only a place somewhere other than the port that they outguarded. The information was enough because it had to be such.

Furgeson deserves close scrutiny. He is the best kind of company leader, the lengthened shadow of which becomes a general. Twenty-eight-year-old, a son of Palmyra, New York, and a product of Alfred University, he is earnest but never painfully so. Through habit, he knows each of his soldiers by name, home town, and background; what happens to any and all of his people in combat, he insists on finding out. This drive comes not of idle curiosity but from determination to learn from one's own mistakes. Furgeson gives his lieutenants and NCO's plenty of head room. They run their own platoons. But more than that, there is this special quality in him, that he puts it as his right to have a full year in the fire line. Furgeson states his case simply: "There is no reason why I should not share the full risks taken by my men." His is an unusual pride even among captains of infantry.

Company strength that morning was 139, and save for about 5 per cent who were newly arrived replacements these were seasoned and hearty soldiers accustomed to stalking the VC by night in the thickets outside Tuy Hoa, doing their hunting in packets of eight. With some help from the Koreans, the battalion had done a first class job of restoring security to the port proper. During the patrolling outside its perimeter, they always traveled light.

This day they went forth loaded for bear. Not knowing what lay ahead, they did not run the risk of running short of fighting supply, or so they thought, though Dong Tre was relatively a short hop from Tuy Hoa. The riflemen carried 280 rounds for their M-16's, 4 frag grenades, and 3 days' rations with 2 canteens apiece. Every other man toted a claymore mine. The thump gunners (M-79 launcher men) carried 59 rounds per person. The RTO's and squad leaders, in addition to weapons and radios, had 5 smoke grenades each. With every M-60 machine gun went 1200 rounds. The load was enough to founder a mule train.

At high noon on 19 June the men of Alpha Company were lifted by Hueys out of Tuy Hoa for the assault and in less than one hour were set down on a prepped (worked over) landing zone atop Hill 98. This ground (at 023-673) had been pounded by six gunships and the artillery based on the crossroads to the east of the hill. All twenty-six Hueys made it easily, touching down six at a time. The hill was covered with waist-high elephant grass; its fairly even slopes had been terraced to slow erosion and the surface was checkered with hedgerows. Though it was wholly formidable to the eye and might have proved a deadfall, it was unmanned and unfortified.

The sun was brutal. Furgeson lost two men to heat prostration before getting beyond the base of the hill.

Apart from that particular misery—the temperature was 104 degrees—they did not anticipate unusual trials. The word had been passed around that a regiment of United States Marines—eighteen hundred men—was being landed from a carrier to the north of Tuy An. The Marines would advance inland with ship fire support from two cruisers and two destroyers. The company's northward march would intercept the regiment's move westward and after the link-up it would be roses, roses all the way, though there was supposed to be a Cong battalion somewhere around Trung Luong.

So the company crunched along, not too unhappy despite the fiery furnace. It had deployed in two columns of two platoons each, separated by about five hundred meters, the scouts keeping an eye peeled for the upcoming Leathernecks that were never to arrive. The Marines, bent on a training mission, under instructions not to engage unless fired on, took thirty-seven casualties from the heat that day and returned otherwise unscathed some time later to the carrier.

Two thousand meters along, PFC John McCorkle, lead scout of the column on the left, saw a helmeted figure in khaki on the trail twenty meters to his front. The Cong had entered the trail on an angle, his side turned, his rifle slung.

McCorkle fired and missed. The Cong scuttled away into the bushes.

McCorkle said words unprintable, as did the men behind him. It is a playlet oft repeated in Vietnam.

Seconds later, First and Third Platoons came under sniper fire. At least, that was what they called it, though the shooting was from far off and the bullets went wide of the mark. There was enough of it, however, to check the company bodily for at least twenty minutes.

Furgeson reasoned that the oblique fire had the purpose of diverting the company from Dinh Phong village, which lay directly ahead. Still, it is not less probable, in view of the sudden appearance of the lone Cong, who could have been a decoy, that the distant marksmen were also lures of an ambush that fortunately missed its game. So Furgeson decided to deploy First and Third Platoons in line to sweep into Dinh Phong.

Through the center of the village ran a shallow creek with a flat bed wide as a city block, this between high banks, a creek that would prove to be bad news for the company. Though it turned out that Dinh Phong was heavily fortified, the sweep was bloodless. Seventeen young men of the village—local VC—were taken into custody. Six rice caches and twenty black uniforms were destroyed.

By the time the work was completed, the hour was 1730. Furgeson decided that it was time to knock off for the day. The CP, with Weapons Platoon and Third outguarding it, went into perimeter at coordinates 024-693. Second Platoon backtracked to set up a trail ambush (029-687) where the lone NVA soldier had been spotted. First Platoon was sent west to ambush along another trail at 015-690.

The night was serenely quiet except for one episode at First Platoon's location that almost mocks belief.

At either end of the ambush the platoon had an M-60 and a radio, while at the center of the position was an unoccupied native hooch. No one had noticed that a second trail diagonally joined the main trail at the far side of the structure.

Private Gary Housley was doing the 0100 to 0200 trick on the machine gun at the extreme left flank. He heard a noise, looked up, and saw the heads of five NVA soldiers bobbing along in clear silhouette twenty meters away and moving toward the hooch. They had come via the unnoticed side trail. Before Housley could move or turn the M-60, the apparitions were swallowed by the darkness next to the house.

Four of them lay down next to the house. The fifth man crawled right in among the Americans doing guard duty. With his elbow, he nudged PFC Gerald Sweeney, who, possibly nodding a bit, had missed his arrival.

Sweeney said: "Heiner, is that you? What do you want?"

Spec 4 Bob Heiner was his partner in the position. He was gently sleeping.

The figure replied: "Hey, how many honchos do we have out here?" The English was good enough, and the accent was broad Brooklynese, just like Heiner's.

Sweeney said: "Repeat the question." He was puzzled, not suspicious.

At that, Heiner came awake and jumped up. Seeing him, Sweeney was too startled to react or even to understand what was happening.

Then all five North Vietnamese jumped up, shoving at one another as they scrambled to get away. They ran directly past the muzzle of Housley's machine gun not more than an arm's length away from it.

The first one yelled: "Hold it! Wait a minute. Be nice now."

So Housley held it. They were too close to him, and the targets were too fleeting in any case.

From the other end of the position, Staff Sergeant Marion Calvert yelled: "Hey, what in the hell is going on down there?" He was already coming on the run and his temper was high.

He barked at Sweeney: "Why in the hell didn't you fire?"

Sweeney replied: "Why should I? I thought they were friendlys."

So far, not a round had been fired.

Then with Calvert still standing in the clear, Housley saw one more Charlie come bobbing along down the side trail. At least, he thought that he was a Charlie. The figure was singing: "Yah, yah, yahdeeah, yah, yah," a pop tune in the United States. Housley held fire.

The figure came to within five feet of Housley, rifle pointed at Housley's head. Almost too late Housley smelled him and saw the bare feet.

Housley's M-16 was on his lap. He raised it very slowly till he reckoned the muzzle was within three feet of the man's chin. Then he pulled the trigger, one bullet only. The figure kicked over backward, almost somersaulting. The bullet made a clean hole.

This was the only blood drawn.

Then both machine guns opened fire for a wasting of ammunition that had no other effect than to waken all sleepers. Calvert called Furgeson to report what had happened.

Furgeson commented: "It begins to look as if they're as mixed up as we are."

At 0830, Furgeson got a call from Colonel Wasco, who told him: "You are to move on and reinforce C Company. Get there as soon as possible."

The only additional information provided him, Furgeson said later, was that C Company was meeting "squad type resistance."

PFC Pardick, the RTO for the artillery forward observer, monitored another conversation at the same time. From the gunner's view, the resistance was of "reinforced platoon size, plus or minus, and more probably plus."

Here was a whale of a difference.

At 0900 Furgeson's company got on the move again and without interruption slogged along fifteen hundred meters due northwest through the hamlet of The Hien. The day was beastly hot and canteens were too soon dry. Directly west of the hamlet about two hundred meters distant was a ridge finger. Taking position on that rise, Furgeson rested the main body for the next thirty minutes, while Second Platoon pushed on another seven hundred meters northwest to check out the hamlet of Trung Luong 2.

Though by this time Furgeson doubted that any fighting lay ahead, he set up one 81-mm. mortar and two machine guns to cover the advance. The men sprawled in the sun, except for the weapons crews. Second Platoon reached the objective without a shot being fired.

Lieutenant Walter E. Eddy called back to Furgeson over the RT: "No trouble here. But there's a fine well of clear water. We can fill our canteens."

Furgeson said: "No. You must push on and establish full security. I'll come up to you. Then you can think about water."

To be on the safe side and make the best use of ground cover, he led his people forward via the creek bed that wound between the finger and the hamlet.

As Eddy had said, there was no trouble. The hamlet was untenanted except for a withered crone who crouched between two of the huts paying them no attention. The well water was sweet, and a small banana grove was popping with ripe fruit on which the soldiers gorged themselves after slaking thirst.

"It sure is quiet here," said Eddy.

"For my money," said Furgeson, "it's too damned quiet."

Eddy and his men moved on to check out a second section of the hamlet. Its size and shape, Furgeson from his position couldn't even guess; the edge was curtained off by a symmetrical hedgerow, three feet thick at the base, which was formed of earth bank and thorn bushes, while from the crown grew a screen of twenty-foot-high bamboo. If the base was fire-slotted, Eddy might be walking into a deadfall.

To Furgeson's south a perfectly flat plain extended for about two hundred meters, after he had pulled his men away from the first group of huts. Unconcerned with that quarter, he returned First Platoon and the command group to the creek bed to continue the advance, following after Eddy. The banks were high, the bottom so tight that two men could not walk abreast.

Furgeson stayed on the bank top to keep Second Platoon in sight. He saw Eddy and the column pass the hedgerow and get on beyond the farthest huts and he felt a great sense of relief.

That was when, as soldiers crudely put it, all hell broke loose beyond the bamboo curtain. From somewhere close to Eddy, who was no longer visible, Furgeson heard the crack and rising rattle of automatic fire in heavy volume. Not knowing what it meant, he was left for the moment in his private lonely limbo, which is the worst part of being a skipper.

Eddy had walked into a point-blank ambush just behind the huts. Quickly the fusillade nailed him. He was hit by several bullets and both legs were shattered. The blow spun him and he disappeared. He had dropped into a four-feet-deep foliage-covered pit, though his platoon was given no time to search for him.

The same outburst of fire had felled his RTO, Spec 4 Johnson. It had wiped out the machine gun crew, PFC Richard J. Hinton, first gunner, PFC Patrick J. Mooney, second gunner, and PFC Alton B. Munn, the ammo bearer. All four men were first hit in the legs. A few minutes later each died with a bullet through the head, before anyone could get up to them.

Before Furgeson could stop him, the company's Senior Aid Man, Spec 4 John Cottin, who was with the main body, sprinted forward to supply first aid. A more impetuous, willing youngster would be hard to imagine. But for the time being he did not go very far. Other men held him back.

In none of this was First Platoon immediately and directly involved. The men were still in the creek bed. The sounds of fire were quite indistinct. Private Housley, the brain working in slow motion, asked: "Do you suppose we are in a fight? Should somebody get up there?" He responded to his own question by starting off.

Three men had already taken off ahead of him. All four of them ran. They had dashed up the bank and were moving over the high ground. From frontward, at the apex of a bend in the creek, an enemy machine gun opened fire, at a range of thirty meters. All four hit the dirt. The bullet stream kicked up dust and pebbles, blinding them. One by one they rolled back down the bank into the creek.

Then they started forward along the bank, figuring that if the gun was sited for the higher level, they could get on its rear with impunity.

PFC Jim Reddy, a machine gunner who was playing lead-off, yelled back: "Hey, look, I see a tree coming toward me."

The second man, PFC John Krebs, cried out: "If you see a tree moving, that's Charlie."

Reddy flopped and opened fire with his M-60.

They had all flopped in the same split second. Housley, who was now the third man, yelled: "I think you got him." But he could not be sure. He had seen the tree fall. But he had also later observed it moving up the ditch.

Seconds, minutes, or at least some interval passed with nothing happening as they lay there.

Housley, who was not more eager than innocent, asked: "Isn't it time to move again?"

Acting Platoon Sergeant Robert d'Amour was made of steadier and less impetuous stuff. He lay in the creek bed flat on his belly, an unlighted cigarette in his mouth.

He called to Housley: "Can't you throw me a light?"

Housley had only a Ronson lighter, a gift from home, but with due respect for rank, he gave it a toss. D'Amour had time to light up, take a few puffs, and toss back the lighter with a "much obliged," a measure of courtesy not usually found in movies or TV tape portraying the way Americans act in war. D'Amour was concerned only with slowing his men down until he got orders.

In this he was foiled. While the lighter was doing its forward pass to Housley, a bullet hit D'Amour directly under the knee cap. He screamed like a Comanche. The men had never heard anything like that from D'Amour, a leader with whom they identified. But then the pain of a wound is each according to his own.

Within five minutes, he was given a shot of morphine. It helped very little. D'Amour said to Housley: "If you would just give me a grenade, I'd blow my damn guts out." Though Housley listened politely, no one was taking D'Amour's bid. They picked him up, pulled back some distance, and went into perimeter next to the shank of the village, waiting and watching to see what would happen next. The men nearest D'Amour were concerned with him and not with the company's problem, at least for this time. The hour was 1030, the richest time of lovely morning, according to poets.

We now get the precipitating action from the viewpoint of an extraordinary witness, PFC Raymond A. Wilson, a twenty-one-year-old Negro from New York City. Wilson had entered the Army from Boston University, where he was a psychology major. But his main interest was not in the world of science. His father is a lieutenant of detectives in the New York force and young Wilson intended to follow in his footsteps. This morning he was getting his first heavy smell of danger at close range.

He was a fire team leader in the first squad; he walked just behind Eddy and had him ever in sight until the big heat began. They had walked a trail that wound through the end of the hamlet and they had not stopped to search the last of the huts, though in the end that oversight counted little.

Next to the trail, where the built-up area gave way to open field, was a large barnlike structure two stories high. As the tail of the column swung past that structure, four bullets, fired one at a time, banged into the upper part of the building. They had come from so far off that Furgeson, three hundred meters to the rear, had missed the sounds altogether. Second Platoon's men, startled, all hit the dirt. Seconds later they arose, feeling sheepish and laughing at one another.

Eddy was sore as a boil. He yelled: "Get moving! What the hell, that guy is way off."

What neither he nor anyone else realized in that moment, crucial above all others, was that this was part of the lure, the beginning of entrapment, a trick that the Congs use time and again, to create the impression that there is game to be sought somewhere in the background, but no immediate danger palpable and present. It will make troops hurry on, and out of rushing comes carelessness.

Young Wilson, for one, could not even think in those terms. They had been in file while on the trail. But as they arose and debouched into the field, Eddy yelled: "Fire teams right and left!" So within less than one minute after the first bullets cracked, they had formed a front and were moving forward quite spread out. Twenty meters directly ahead of the point men were three small, innocent-looking haystacks.

Then it happened.

Fire was all around them. It "seemed to come from everywhere," or at least from both flanks and rear. And it was flat and mighty close.

Wilson heard cries of "Medic! Medic!" The calls came from the point men, PFC's James Brown, Robert L. Westover, and Ronald W. Sander. All had been hit.

Eddy came running back, and as he passed Wilson he yelled, "Take cover! Take cover!" No need to say it. Everybody was down. Just missing him, a burst of bullets smashed into a stump next Wilson.

Eddy bounded on. He had almost reached the big barn when another burst of bullets caught him around both knees and he vanished into the hole. Wilson was no longer paying attention to Eddy. Grenades were exploding all around him and he was hugging earth face down.

Brown came crawling back, yelling, "We got men hit up front." He was bleeding around the head. Then as if suddenly aware of what his words meant, Brown turned about and crawled forward again to help attend the wounded.

Off to the right about twenty meters, a hedge ran parallel to the line on which they had advanced. Mooney, the gunner, crawled that way, looking for Eddy. He was calling: "Lieutenant! Lieutenant!" As he got within five feet of the hedge, a Cong leaned over it and shot him through the head. Mooney dragged himself back and died sprawled across his machine gun. Hinton, a new boy in the company having his first day of battle, stood up to stare at Mooney, as if puzzled by the sight of death, or waiting for a bullet to drive into his front. The Cong shot him and he died in the same way as Mooney with a bullet through his head, a quite useless sacrifice. If he had to be shot, it was no break to see it coming. Munn was killed near the other two, probably by the same Cong, while approaching the hedge. No one saw him fall.

Not more than three or four minutes had passed. No one in the platoon was fighting back; not one round had been fired from the ground where these men lay. No one tried to give orders. The unit was down and desolated. Private Wilson wondered dully whether anyone was getting the word back to the company. But it didn't occur to him to try, as is so often the case during battle's first shock. The field continued fire-swept, though —except for the Cong who had leaned over the hedge—no sign of a live enemy was to be seen.

The killing fire that had downed Second Platoon had come from under the haystacks. They were mere camouflage, topping off three concrete bunkers, fixed with fire slots, armed with light machine guns, and equipped with field telephones. Not one thing in the field had indicated the existence of a military position anywhere nearby. The ground had not been tramped over; the grass was not beaten down. Not one foxhole marred the surface. The appearance of innocence had deceived the platoon completely.

Only one factor had saved Second Platoon from being wiped out. Overexcited about their opportunity, the Charlies at first fired too low. Still, the hurt from that first volleying was hard enough. PFC Jessie Edwards, Private Elbert Jones, Spec 4 George Weary, PFC William L. Sims, and PFC Norbell R. Wright were all casualties from the initial blast, and each of these men had taken leg wounds.

All that Captain Furgeson knew for certain in these first few minutes was that radio contact with Second Platoon had been lost without one ominous word being spoken. He had to guess what he could from that. Eddy must be down. His RTO must be hit, also. Either that, or a first round had smashed the PRC-25. This last seemed unlikely.

All things added up and there could only be one answer.

Furgeson said loudly: "Ambush, just another god-damned ambush."

Like every other rifle commander in Vietnam, he loathed the word and the realization was bitter as gall. His advance party had been suckered.

Furgeson got on his RT to Third Platoon, saying: "We've lost contact with Second. We got to get up there. Start moving."

Receiving the message was the Platoon RTO, an extraordinary eighteen-year-old from Morristown, New Jersey, PFC Joseph C. Comazzi. A physical giant and all-around athlete who had starred in wrestling and high hurdles, Comazzi was experiencing his first day in combat and relishing it all the way, much to his surprise.

Comazzi yelled out the command to the others. The headquarters group, including Furgeson, was already in motion, going forward at a jog. Both groups advanced to the last buildings next to the edge of the field, and stopped there, covered by the hedgerow that hemmed the rear of the hamlet.

Furgeson deployed into the big barn and from its second story positioned an M-60 to fire across the field out of a window. He still had no awareness of the bunkers. Comazzi posted another M-60 on the first floor, then placed three men in a lean-to adjoining the barn to outguard against any movement around the line's right flank. The rest of the men had already spread out behind the parallel hedgerow.

The riflemen were not yet firing, however. Second Platoon's wounded men, and some of its able-bodied, were spread out over the ground forward of the hedge, lying flat and waiting for deliverance, thereby prohibiting fire until Third Platoon's men could be certain that the casualties had been cleared. From the big barn, the two machine guns worked over the haystacks, the lower one firing through a break in the hedge. That was enough help to make Second Platoon a little mobile again; a few of the wounded came crawling from the field under their own power.

Comazzi came out of the big barn and, covered by the parallel hedge, walked leftward about ten meters. This brought him to a break in the hedge bank, through which ran the path that Second Platoon had taken. He could hear a man screaming. The voice was Eddy's though Comazzi did not know it. Peering over the hedge, he could see Mooney's body, and he felt something halfway between a chill and a sweat. He could also see a PRC-25 a few feet from Mooney, still seemingly in working condition.

From the other side of the hedge came a cry: "We need help. Come help us!" It was the voice of Sergeant Pedro Escarillo, a twenty-year-old Mexican from Monterrey, Coahuila. As do most Mexicans who join the United States Army, Escarillo had status in the company as a good combat hand. He was down now, with a bullet through the back. Comazzi did not know it was Escarillo calling. They had never met. The voice was just that of another American in distress. Or so he thought.

So Comazzi, the hurdler, took a running jump and went over the hedge. Right behind him was Sergeant Ernesto Martinez, the platoon leader, though Martinez had slipped through a gap in the hedge. Going at all was their mistake.

Thirty meters on they saw a haystack. Somewhere up there a voice was calling. So they went for the stack. Whereas they should have been killed during the sprint, both were within ten meters of the stack when the machine gun opened fire. They hit the dirt and the bullet stream zinged over their heads.

Comazzi felt no reaction other than wonderment that he was still unhurt and a self-questioning about what to do next. He slipped off on his belly to the perpendicular hedgerow on his right, the same bank that had afforded cover to the Cong who had killed Mooney. Then he stood atop the hedgerow in plain sight and from this flanking position emptied two clips from his M-16 into the side of the closest haystack, hitting it just above ground level. Though it was one of the boldest acts of the day, Comazzi wasn't trying to play Mr. Big. Stunting or playing hero wouldn't even occur to him. He is just by nature a man unafraid, a type of warrior who is very rare indeed.

Next he heard Martinez calling: "Will you help me with fire

so I can get out of here?" The sergeant, who did not yet know Comazzi by name, remained flattened in front of the stack. Comazzi shifted his fire to the front of the stack. Martinez arose, ran, and dove over the same hedge head first.

Comazzi fell back and joined him behind the earth bank. Together, from behind this protecting barrier they poured fire into the several stacks. This done, they crawled back along the far side of the hedge to a point where, frontally, from an oblique angle, they could train fire on the mouths of the concealed bunkers and neutralize them while other men of Third Platoon left their cover along the parallel hedge to rescue Eddy from his predicament. So far they had done nothing to help Escarillo directly, though that character managed to wiggle rearward while Eddy was being lifted from the hole. Still, they felt enormously satisfied with themselves, this two-man fire team. And so they should have been. Together they had discovered and exposed the main enemy position.

Mooney's body was still sprawled across his gun. Someone from Third Platoon crawled through the hedge gap to Mooney, grabbed his jacket, and rolled him off the gun. Then this self-starter put the body on a poncho and dragged it back to the big barn.

Mortar fire was now ranging in on the big barn and the house next door. Furgeson kept shifting between the two, his RTO in one place, some of his wounded in the other. Several hundred meters to the rear, his XO, Lieutenant Jonathan Towers, an Australian-reared native of England, was monitoring the explosions on his radio. The more he listened, the more Towers felt the urge to get forward. So he quit Weapons Platoon and came on the run, followed by Aid Man John Cottin.

With no one trying to stop him, Towers bounded right on through the gap in the parallel hedge. From within the house, Furgeson heard the bang of a mortal shell exploding just outside and a little short of the building. Then he heard Towers' voice on the RT: "Got me! I say, I been hit. Smarts a bit. I mean it hurts like hell."

Unhelped, Towers crawled back through the hedge. Then he arose and walked to the front stoop of the house that was serving as the CP, there to seat himself a trifle unsteadily.

Sergeant Richard C. Snyder said to him: "You better get inside the house."

Towers shook him off, paying no attention.

Spec 4 Joe Amaya, a medic, made his try. "Lieutenant, did you know that besides that slug in your shoulder you've been hit in the backside also?"

Towers asked: "Really?" and moved into the house.

Furgeson greeted him with: "And that's what you get for being an eager beaver." Towers felt a bit forlorn. Wounded, he was getting no sympathy anywhere.

His wounds having been dressed by Amaya and feeling no compassion directed toward him in this quarter, Towers, to everyone's amazement, took off for a job in his rearward post and resumed his work as XO, bringing in medevac ships and regulating the flow of ammo and water forward.

His winning of a Purple Heart had been somewhat less than heroic. He had charged, bled, and recoiled, without doing anyone any good.

More mournful still was the consequence of the charge of Aid Man John Cottin. The twenty-year-old from Los Angeles had tarried in the CP while Towers entered upon the field. He now enigmatically stayed there when Towers took off for the rear, Cottin possibly feeling that his duty lay forward.

Then in a trice, he was gone. Furgeson saw him dart for the door and shouted, "John!" meaning to detain him. But Furgeson was a second or so too late.

Comazzi, from his position behind the perpendicular hedge, saw Cottin come on through the gap in the hedge that bounded the big barn. Comazzi tried to shout him down above the din. From his position between the big barn and the parallel hedge, PFC Michael L. Pardick, nineteen, of Richmond, California, who had come along with the company as FO for the artillery, could hear Comazzi's voice ring out loud and clear: "Get down, for God's sake, get down!"

Cottin kept going. As he hit the ground, then got to his knees, he yelled back: "No Charlie will ever kill me." Then he bent over to apply mouth-to-mouth resuscitation to a soldier Comazzi knew was already dead.

Comazzi watched hypnotized by the futility of it all. Even as Cottin leaned forward and came almost face to face with the corpse, he was kicked backward by a bullet that got him through the heart.

So died, wholly uselessly, an aid man beloved by his comrades and of whom a devoted mother wrote: "John believed that life was beautiful, for at twenty he was still naive and trusting. To him each new day was a new world."

Comazzi wended his way back to the big barn to tell the others that Cottin was dead. Before he could break the news, something else distracted him. Inside the barn an old Vietnamese woman squatted in a corner where a rude fireplace joined the wall. She was wailing loudly, but doing it in fits and starts. The wailing got to Comazzi's nerves; it sounded too much like a put-on. At last he picked her up bodily and locked her in a tool closet.

Minutes later, PFC Brown, from his position alongside the parallel hedge, saw a camouflaged figure with a rifle (it was a U.S. M-16) in its right hand emerge from the chimney atop the big barn and lower itself down on the roof. Taking a chance, Brown emptied half a clip into the man. The figure rolled over and over, then plunged, the plummeting body barely missing Furgeson, who had popped from the doorway to see what the shooting was about.

A sudden light dawned on Comazzi, who had followed Furgeson out the door. The sniper had been in the chimneytop all along. The wailing hag had been signaling him.

On impulse, Comazzi started for the tool closet to yank her out, thought better of it, then reeled through the door on the other side and walked to the rear about forty meters. His stomach churning from nausea, he felt that he must get away from the fight for at least a few minutes.

The field quieted. Some instinct told Furgeson that the enemy had pulled back from the ambush line under the haystacks. Very probably the North Vietnamese began looking for a chance to pull back after Comazzi and Martinez had turned the heat on.

Furgeson waited, maybe five minutes. Not one round was fired. Then leading the CP group, Furgeson moved through the gap in the hedge and advanced to the nearest haystack. Next to the stack, they flopped. It was the new CP.

Soon over the PRC-25 Furgeson was in contact with Staff Sergeant Marion D. Calvert of Second Platoon.

Furgeson asked: "Do you know whether you now have all of your wounded? Are you in shape to pull back?"

Calvert replied: "I am not sure. I can't get contact with number one squad that was forward to check it out. But I think one wounded guy is still out there."

Furgeson asked for the wounded man's name and got it.

Furgeson is a little nearsighted and in the rush forward he had lost his glasses. He now peered around the haystack to see if there was a body in sight forward. He was certain he saw one. It was lying about thirty meters to the front. He thought he could hear calls for help coming from that quarter.

There was only one thing to do and out of impulse came his decision. Instead of crawling belly-down to the casualty, he would do it in one dash.

He went like a runner stealing home plate and he closed with a headfirst slide à la Hal Chase, arms forward to clutch at the object. It was a dead sure thing; he knew he had made it—had done it under fire. Then as his hands gripped and he got the feel of things, he found he had embraced, not a human form, but the stump of a long-dead tree.

From rearward, he heard a yell: "What in hell is the Captain doing?"

Pardick, who had yelled, was galvanized by the spectacle. He heard a machine gun open fire and saw bullets kick up dust all around Furgeson, and he reckoned that the captain was dead.

Furgeson lay flat for all of one minute, wondering what to do next. The machine gun, boring straight at him, was thwarted only by the thickness of the stump that Furgeson had mistaken for a man. Chips were flying all about.

Furgeson said softly to himself: "Well, I'll be a sonofabitch." Who wouldn't?

But clearly the thing could not last and no one gets an MH, DSC, or SS for good intentions. It is not heroic to succor a stump.

Pardick saw Furgeson arise, run a few feet, and jump about ten feet toward the hedge on the right. Just then a rocket exploded dead on the stump where Furgeson had been. Furgeson dove through the hedge and collided with one of his soldiers, who had been shot in the arm. To add insult to injury, this was the same man he had risked his life to rescue.

Wholly exasperated, Furgeson asked: "Can you move? Can you talk? Can you do anything?"

The soldier answered: "Yes, sir. Yes, sir."

Then Furgeson cursed him and cursed him hard. His words would not make this narrative any better reading, though by the standards of American book critics, it would make the tale more realistic.

Together they beat it back to the big barn, using the cover of the hedge, at which point Furgeson dropped the recalcitrant soldier and returned to the haystack. So altogether, he had made a 360-degree sortie and had wasted about twenty minutes, which knowledge didn't make him feel any better. However, Pardick felt better when he looked around and saw Furgeson just behind him.

Furgeson was reflecting. Off and on, he had been talking to Colonel Wasco at battalion. There seemed to be little sense in the exercise. Now it was looking more futile than ever. The company was just spinning its wheels and losing too many men, and of what lay in front of him, he, Furgeson, knew no more than before.

So he called Wasco and told him: "I'm going to pull back and put arty and air on this village and the fields beyond it. After that, maybe we'll know what to do."

There was no objection from Wasco, a battalion CO who, despite a personal toughness of soul, respects the judgments of his company commanders.

Without harassment, the company withdrew only as far as the ground held by Towers and the Weapons Platoon. All dead and wounded were cleared from the field. By this time Towers, the Australian, was heads-up and acting as if his wounds had simply solidified his natural strengths. The dust-off choppers were coming into the village and evacuating the wounded. Second and First Platoons were on guard along the hedgerow abounding the village. The Third Platoon had been wheeled farther rearward to take up a guard position along the ridge finger from which the attack had been launched.

Furgeson reckoned that the company role for the rest of the day (it was now passing noon) would be, at worst, one of fending off counterattack. His losses had been fairly crippling. Besides, the hedgerows and houses, and the piecemeal manner of the deployment, were quite disunifying and practically defied reorganization at the scene. He might have reformed on the haystacked field, but so doing would have offered too broad a target to the enemy mortars. In staying there at all the company had found the field costly enough; twenty more of his men were out from heat prostration. Furgeson felt that the less than a hundred who remained to the company were in tolerably good shape and could go again, if pressed. But he would spare them that if he could. The day was too hot, the enemy much too clever; fighting in a hamlet was much too sticky. So ran his thoughts. What bugged him most was that aside from the one fiddler on the roof and the Cong executioner behind the hedgerow, his company had seen no enemy soldiers in the combat zone.

His men were troubled about other things. Pardick had felt that his comrades were "badly shaken up" when the withdrawal was ordered. Yet when they got to the ridge finger morale zoomed again. The men were laughing and joking with one another. It was as if the day had produced nothing untoward. Rations were broken out. For the first time since early morning men felt hungry.

Private Wilson, the budding policeman, was harassed by other worries. The performance of the company had dismayed him. Too many packs and some weapons had been left behind when the men had departed the forward ground.

Belatedly, Wilson, the Good Soldier, the psychologist, and worrier, became aware that his own pack and M-16 were missing, and he could not remember at first where he had left either item. Maybe it was the heat. Also, too much ammunition had been shot off just for the hell of it with no real target in sight.

Then Wilson, a little late, recollected. The packs and weapons had been dropped when the order came through to direct main attention to the evacuation of the wounded. Wilson sweated hard about this, and sweating, remembered more.

He had seen his own weapon and pack propped next to the big barn when he came out. The impression on his brain was indelible; he could remember exactly how they looked. But something had gone wrong with his motor impulses. The brain had flashed no signal to the rest of him: "Those are yours, so carry them out." Out of embarrassment, he was learning something about how the brain functions only halfway when pressure is intense and the heat is high.

In the hamlet, men swarmed like bees around the sweet water well, drinking their fill, and soaking their pates and blouses. Some of them dozed off in the shadows thrown by the huts and hedges. Even ten minutes of sleep will restore a beaten soldier in such circumstances.

The left-behind packs and rifles had not, in fact, been lost. Other riflemen had carried them out, thinking they belonged to the casualties. They had been loaded aboard the choppers under the same supposition, and along with the wounded, were already airborne for Tuy Hoa.

Furgeson laid on two air strikes, six jets, three at a time, as soon as he got to the ridge finger. Then he called for the artillery. "Give me everything you've got!" The shelling of the ground they had fought over, and the fields beyond, continued from 1315 until 1400.

Then he heard from Wasco: "You're to go back in there; they figure all resistance has been knocked off."

Comazzi, who was learning fast, remarked: "The people back there somewhere who can't see the field are really hip."

TRY, TRY AGAIN

WHEN FURGESON and his beat-up line jumped off again at 1410, the formation was notably short of officer-leaders and senior NCO's had largely taken over for lack of any alternative.

Back at the Tuy Hoa base, Wasco was grabbing cooks, mechanics, and clerks for use as rifle replacements and collaring whatever spare lieutenants were in reach. Wasco stayed between a chill and a sweat out of the need to keep his airlift so balanced that time would not be lost in getting casualties out and rushing the able-bodied forward. There was no way to maintain equilibrium, the lift was too short.

Aware that his men were pretty well bushed, Furgeson told them to drop all packs and heavy equipment, leaving the heavy stuff with Weapons Company, which would hold a fall-back base between the ridge finger and the village.

When Furgeson told Wasco over the RT about this decision, Wasco commented: "Okay, but I want that whole village before nightfall."

Furgeson answered: "Fair enough. I'm not worrying about the village. It's what's beyond."

This was not exactly an inspired exchange; despite all the bumps that had been taken, both men were swapping wishes.

The artillery rolled a barrage ahead of the attacking line all the way to the built-up area, the shells breaking about a hundred meters in front of the walking riflemen.

For this time around, Third Platoon led off, followed by First and then Second, the most depleted outfit. They moved not more than 120 meters from the line of departure and there they were stopped when fire broke out from front and flanks.

That body check almost coincided with the touchdown of Wasco's command bird. Wasco was bringing three replacement lieutenants to the action.

They were a mixed bag. Marvin Roberts was a new man. Abe Martin, who should have been a jokesmith all the way, was pushing his luck. He was just two days short of leaving for home, his year completed. As for Dan J. Hill, a Las Vegan and the son of a professional NCO, he had known little except the Army through his life and had enlisted at fifteen years of age in the U.S. infantry.

Wasco had waved them on, saying: "You all get things straightened out," though what needed straightening hadn't been said. It was all the introduction they got.

Hill saw an NCO flattened and asked him: "Who's in command of this company?"

The man said: "Furgeson."

Hill saw an antenna standing clear in the foreground and the three men dashed for it.

His was a good guess. Furgeson greeted them: "Jesus Christ, I'm glad to see you guys," then added: "You get with One, Two, and Three Platoons," pointing to them one at a time and indicating the location of the platoons with other gestures.

Hill moved at once to his people. They seemed jittery. One sergeant next to him said: "We're all shot up."

Hill answered: "Don't worry about it; we got everything made," then turning to his RTO he whispered: "The fact of the matter is that I'm scared shitless." Then he laughed.

Now genuinely worried, Hill returned to Furgeson to say: "We got to do something, go forward or backward and I don't give a damn which, but do something."

Furgeson replied: "We go forward; we'll try again to make it along the creek."

So the line started again and almost as quickly became flattened. Trouble popped in Third Platoon, which, cut to two squads, stretched all the way from the path to the creek bank. The new lieutenant, Abe Martin, who was built like a professional fullback, had spent the interlude trying to jolly his men.

As they moved out, PFC David C. Kranig, a thump gunner, was a few feet ahead of the other men.

First Platoon, under Lieutenant Roberts, was deployed in about the same way on the right side of the creek. The line had advanced over this same ground in the morning attack without incident. So no resistance at close range had been anticipated.

From Comazzi's back at least three automatic weapons opened fire right along the gut of the ravine. Everyone hit the dirt. Seconds later, from forward, out of a break in the creek bank, a machine gun opened fire, not more than twenty meters from the line of skirmishers. So they had walked right into it, an ambush set to box in their deployment over the morning route.

Sergeant Snyder was far over on the left flank, which put him on the high ground, while obscuring his view of what was happening to the men working along the creek bank.

Snyder sang out, "Keep moving! That's nothing. We're not hurt. Get up and go!" He had the little learning that is a dangerous thing.

Kranig, the thump gunner, had taken the blow dead on—bullets in both legs and more bullets in the abdomen. Now he was on his knees, looking back at the others and crying: "They've hit me; you gotta help me."

Then he pitched over, face forward.

Abe Martin and Comazzi were kneeling about twenty meters to Kranig's rear. Martin dashed for Kranig and squatted to look him over.

Martin was given about two seconds for his quick-see, then two bullets got him in the right leg, not just nipping it, but ripping it lengthwise.

The machine gun then put seven more bullets into Kranig. Both soldiers—and Kranig was as large as Martin—became wholly immobilized .

The aid man of the platoon, called "Doc" like the rest of them, PFC Ramon Zamona, a Mexican, sighed, "Boy, I gotta help them but somebody else has got to help me."

Comazzi told him, "Doc, up the creek is just the wrong way to go."

Together, Comazzi and Zamona wiggled on their bellies up the creek bank, through a dried rice paddy, and then down the bank again to come out behind Martin, and they were staying mighty low.

Zamona, just over five feet and weighing about 130 pounds in fair weather, said to Martin, "Sir, I have to help Kranig first; he's worse hurt than you are."

At that point Zamona felt more harassed than a three-legged dog with flees.

Martin replied, "But I'm in terrible pain; I think both legs are broken."

So the Doc gave Martin a shot of morphine and wiggled along to Kranig.

The bandaging of Kranig completed, Zamona was again put on the spot when Kranig protested, "You gotta give me morphine; you gave it to the lieutenant."

Zamona replied with dignity, "That's against orders; you have a stomach wound."

Kranig grunted and did a little cussing.

Moments later, the Mexican relented and gave Kranig the shot.

To ease his conscience, the aid man turned aside to Comazzi and whispered, "What's the difference? The guy is going to die anyway."

A heroic figure, Zamona proved to be a bum diagnostician. There was plenty of life in Kranig. That afternoon he was medevacked to Tuy Hoa in an unconscious state. At the hospital Sergeant Thomas Sandusky looked him over and said, "Don't bother about this guy—he's dead."

Kranig opened his eyes and answered, "I'll be damned if I am!" And he still lives on.

From rearward, Furgeson was trying to raise Lieutenant Martin on the RT. Comazzi answered the call on Martin's RT, saying: "I'm Three Gulf."

That angered Furgeson who bit it off: "Get the hell off the RT. I want Three Six." (That would be Third Platoon's commander.)

The dialogue continued.

Commazzi: "He's WIA."

Furgeson: "How bad?"

Comazzi: "Shot in the leg."

Furgeson: "That's not bad; put him on."

Comazzi: "Can you talk, sir?" (This to Martin.)

Martin: "Can't even think. You do the talking."

Comazzi: "Captain, it's thicker than shit up here."

Furgeson: "OK, boy, slow down, please take it easy."

Comazzi: "Will do. We're going to make poncho litters. I think we can get them back to the CP."

As Comazzi broke off the conversation with Furgeson, Martin said: "This bandage is doing no good and it's hurting like hell."

Comazzi crawled up to him, belly-down.

Furgeson was already in a bind and felt it tightening second by second. His attack was being held up by the downing of only a couple of men. The enemy-stopping weapons were pretty much isolated by the creek bank. And delay to an infantry line, once it is stopped by fire, and even though the damage is slight, depletes its energy.

There was also the risk that if he tarried too long, the resistance might build up before he could get to the village, though the rolling gunfire was some insurance against the possibility. The longer he waited, the more acute became the dillemma.

Getting to Martin, Comazzi found the lieutenant's right pant leg drenched with blood. He whipped out a sheath knife and cut away the cloth at the thigh. Then he could see that the wound was not a simple puncture, but had ripped the length of the leg.

He yelled to Zamona, who was again working on Kranig: "Doc, throw me a bandage."

Zamona tossed him a whopping bandage and as it sailed through the air, Martin looked at it, groaned, and murmured: "That's a hell of a big bandage. I can't be that bad hurt."

Comazzi replied: "Nothing is ever as bad as you think, sir, and besides you got to take what I can give you."

Comazzi pushed the bandage into the wound and still the wound wasn't covered.

PFC Donald Myers cut four bamboo poles for litters; the bamboo grew right there in the creek bed. PFC Richard Wade came forward to help him. Together, using ponchos, they completed the two lifts. It was an interval of quiet; seemingly the enemy had faded back.

Together the four able-bodied men—Comazzi and Zamona had become stretcher bearers—struggled with their heavy burdens, moving them a few feet at a time. They got around a small bend in the creek bank; other soldiers from the platoon were sprawled there.

At that point, the machine gun and AK-47's behind them resumed fire.

Myers sang out: "Somebody's gotta stop that."

Kranig piped up: "Come on you gents. Heads up! You're airborne. You can't let those guys beat you."

Comazzi said: "Listen to the guy talk. Must be that shot you gave him, Doc."

Meanwhile the right flank of Lieutenant Roberts' platoon, which joined Martin's in the creek bed, had become compromised and stalled in almost identical fashion. The men had been wading along through water that was about knee-deep and foully stagnant.

PFC Gary J. Housley, twenty-two, of Tremonton, Utah, was acting as RTO for Platoon Sergeant Calvert, with the extra task of being the contact man charged with keeping the two flanks joined. Next him on the right walked Sergeant Reinier W. Biliowski.

With the first burst of machine-gun fire, Biliowski took a bullet through the stomach.

He dropped into the water.

Housley dove behind an earth bulge in the creek bank.

Calvert yelled: "Get a machine gun up here and start firing to cover Biliowski."

No one responded.

All of the men had scrambled for such cover as could be found in the earth folds of the banks on either side. There is no proof that any machine gunner heard what Calvert had said.

Five or so minutes passed. An M-60 gun, PFC Richard Montgomery carrying it, was brought forward and put in position to leftward of Housley—in other words, on the other side of the creek bank. Montgomery barely got started firing; a bullet from the enemy machine gun drilled him through the right knee.

Housley, who was from the other platoon, pulled Montgomery to cover behind another earth bulge in the bank. The same aid man who had startled Lieutenant Towers in the morning, Joe Amaya, crawled forward to see if he could help Montgomery. The enemy machine gun was still firing straight down the gut of the creek bed and men managed to get forward only by hugging the banks.

With the bullet stream passing directly above the body of Biliowski, who was lying in the water, no one moved up to attempt his extrication. So for minutes he lay there at dead center of the creek bed, the main target, spared only because so little of him was to be seen above the water, while at the same time the two good Samaritans worked on Kranig and Martin next to the bank, directly to his left.

One of Third Platoon's M-60's was shifted to the bank in an attempt to quiet the enemy gun, but it couldn't begin to bear on the position. The small bamboo thicket was in the way. PFC James E. Cromer, a thump gunner, thought he might blast through the growth by giving it a few M-79 rounds. After one round, his launcher would not function. Out of sheer rage and frustration, Cromer pulled out his Colt .45 and emptied it into the thicket.

All of this was getting to Sergeant Bobby Carter. He stripped off his webbed gear and shouted: "I'm going in and pull him out."

Carter did a dance along the creek bed, zigzagging through the water, in a try to cheat the fire. It didn't work. The bullet swarm followed him, his legs gave out, he fell, and then gave up the quest, lucky enough that he could return unscathed. Later in the day he was not so lucky; both hands were blown off in a grenade accident.

From up creek an enemy AT gun opened fire and with its first two rounds knocked out Third Platoon's machine gun. Things were fast going to hell in a hand basket. The crewmen, PFC's Gallon P. Brown and Robert P. Lettman, were both badly wounded.

Next, from high ground directly to right of the company and

not more than thirty meters above the creek bank, a sniper opened fire, enfilading the line. A group of soldiers went scrabbling to the rear, dragging with them PFC Montgomery, the boy with the wounded knee. Though the pain must have been terrible, he did not cry out.

At about this time, with the bullet stream shifting elsewhere, Biliowski, who had stripped off his pack and dropped his weapon, started to crawl down the creek. As he got in motion, a second enemy machine gun opened fire on him.

Sergeant Floyd C. Denson was crawling along the top of the bank from Third Platoon's ground, looking for a point where he could get parallel with Biliowski, make a running jump rightward, and pull him out.

As Denson crawled, he yelled: "Give him smoke!" Several men tossed out grenades and quickly the creek trench was billowing beautifully with crimson and violet clouds.

Denson pushed on. Just as he came even with Biliowski and was about to take the plunge, a machine-gun burst got him through the head and neck and he died instantly.

From behind the smokescreen Cromer and Lieutenant Roberts went in to get Biliowski. They made it all right, dragging him from the water and up the bank on the left, where Denson had died.

As Cromer pulled him over the verge, another machine-gun bullet creased the back of Biliowski's skull. The same burst hit Cromer in the right arm and leg and he toppled into a foxhole.

Roberts had slipped and fallen into a cleft halfway up the bank. He was now standing and yelling: "Give us smoke! Give us smoke!" More red was thrown, and this time some green.

Under its cover, Roberts moved to get Denson, under the impression that the sergeant was still alive. Discovering his mistake, he still pulled out rearward, dragging the body.

Then Roberts started back for Cromer, though bullets were kicking up dirt all around him.

Together, Housley and Calvert crawled forward, also pointing for Cromer. They could hear Cromer calling: "God damn it, don't forget me. Don't leave me out here."

Housley called: "Don't worry, we're coming to get you."

Roberts was now walking boldly up the trail, acting like a man who didn't care to live very long, blasting with his M-16 as he moved.

Yet that fire, if not helping Housley and Calvert, made the two men feel very good. They wiggled right along the bank, reached down, grabbed Cromer by his wrists, yanked him from the hole, and dragged him back to the casualty collection point just off the trail, in defilade, a hundred meters to the rear. Cromer made no complaint; he was glad enough to get going.

Biliowski had just reached the collection point.

Snyder looked down at him. He said: "Somebody do something for Biliowski."

The aid man, Moore, replied: "I can't; there's nothing that can be done."

Biliowski opened his eyes, gave one great gasp, and died.

So the ordeal in his behalf had all been for nothing. In fact, the whole mournful show, lasting just a little more than one hour from first to last curtain, had been for nothing. There were fourteen wounded and two dead to show for the wasted afternoon.

Soon the medevac Hueys began to arrive. First Sergeant Leon M. Rader, thirty-two, of Knoxville, Tennessee, had called for them earlier. The first three wounded were put aboard. Just then another machine gun opened fire from somewhere out on the left front. One bullet hit a door gunner, and with that, the choppers took off, leaving the other casualties behind.

Furgeson wasn't given time to worry about that. Fire was now coming at him from the rear. Second Platoon, which had been detailed to clear away the casualties, was ordered to drop all of that. Instead, with Lieutenant Hill leading, it would do a mop-up on the hamlets to the rear.

By 1730, Hill had cleaned out the first two of them, killing seven VC and taking as many prisoners during the sweep. Young Wilson, the psychologist who aspired to be a policeman, had killed three of the varmints, besides capturing a machine gun.

Furgeson called Wasco, gave him a full account of the afternoon's failure, and asked for permission to withdraw.

Wasco said: "Go ahead."

Two more medevac ships had come in and cleared away all of the breakage except Biliowski's body. So for the company it was back to the same ridge finger again, this time carrying the dead man.

Quite late on that very dark night, using flashlights, they loaded Biliowski aboard another Huey for his last ride out.

This one was a night for flashlights. Throughout the bivouac troops could see scores of them winking on and off in the hamlets forward and on the back trails winding up the ridges far to the north. Furgeson could only guess what it meant. The hamlet activity could mean either withdrawal or reinforcement. The lights on the high ground suggested carrying parties taking out casualties.

Furgeson called for artillery to lay on fires, which was done, but as to range, it was a wild guess.

There were several long talks with Wasco over the RT.

Furgeson said: "If I have to go back in there, I'd like to do it at night."

Wasco said: "Don't worry; there's no thought about sending you in a third time."

At some time during this same night, the overall operation was given its code name, "Nathan Hale," in honor of the man who had only one life to give to his country.

Two more battalions from the First Cavalry Division were

lifted into the fighting zone, one of them landing next the cross-roads near Dong Tre. Getting the news, Furgeson felt none too cheerful about Wasco's assurances.

At 0900 Wasco flew into the position.

Furgeson gave him a quick rundown, concluding with: "This company is really worn down; by now, we've taken twenty-eight heat casualties."

Wasco said: "Hang loose till I give you the word; you are now under First Cavalry control. But you will just be used in a blocking role."

Said Furgeson: "You want to bet on that?"

Comazzi, talking to Housley at the same time, was saying: "I'm sore in every part of my body. If we go in again, I'm almost sure to get it. But I still think we ought to go."

Housley drily remarked: "Don't try to play tiger."

At 0915, resupply as well as replacements came flooding in. The replacements consisted of twenty-seven new riflemen who the day before at base camp had been working as cooks, mechanics, bakers, and clerks, quite content to stay that way. With them was a strange lieutenant, Scaglioni, an eager G5 working for MACV, at Saigon.

Scaglioni faced north, made a sweep of his arms toward the hamlets and ridges, and said: "Jeez, I'd like to be out there."

It was hardly the best way to start.

Wasco answered: "If you're that full of fight, you can sure get with it."

Furgeson said: "Welcome to the command of the Third Platoon."

Rader, the first sergeant who had sounded the alarm for the medevac Hueys, just stood on the sidelines and grinned like Tweedledee.

A RARE DAY
IN JUNE

HIGH command seemed to be having trouble making up its mind.

At 1015 Furgeson asked that an air strike be laid on the village at 1100.

At 1045 there came a call from Wasco: "You will move out just as quickly as possible and attack the village again."

So the air attack had to be diverted elsewhere.

Moreover, the way it was put to Furgeson, Alpha Company was not being called on this time to go it alone. One platoon of the battalion's Charley Company would attack toward the village from the line of the creek near the sugarloaf hill. And Charley Company, First Battalion, Eighth Cavalry, lifted to the ridge north of the village, would zap the enemy from the high ground. Planned as a three-way squeeze, it sounded beautiful.

Furgeson stayed skeptical. He had long since learned the first lesson of field soldiering: "Don't expect too much."

The day was stifling, blistering hot, the worst heat of a trying summer. The place was furiously beset by bugs of all kinds, which pestilence, like the temperature, hung heaviest around the creek. When the order came to move, men got to their feet as if their own weight was as troublesome as their fighting burdens.

Furgeson lined them up for the attack just as they had gone in the afternoon before. First Platoon, which had almost staked out a claim on the creek bed, would go that way again.

As they stood there, ready to jump off, a flight of Sky Raiders (A-1E's) came over and Furgeson decided to hold up the attack for a few minutes while they had a go at the village. It might help a bit and couldn't possibly do any harm.

The first run by the four Sky Raiders was north to south and by the end of it they had splashed a curtain of napalm not more than one hundred meters in front of the company, and plastered the village with 250-pound bombs. Then they made their passes from east to west, continuing for the next twenty minutes and popping smoke as they flew. These were good strikes, accurately laid on, and they achieved something besides intensifying the natural heat of the day with all the smoking and burning.

Again, Furgeson had asked for a rolling barrage, and the gunners had done their part well, keeping the shells breaking about fifty meters out in front of the advancing line.

First Platoon was again moving via the creek bed, and had reached its point of farthest advance along that alley. The other flank was up to the first line of the huts of the hamlet.

Then staggering along the path came ten North Vietnamese soldiers, their hands in the air. Three were waving white flags. The Americans held fire. The NVA's were neatly dressed in new khaki uniforms but had taken quite a beating in the air strike. Three of them were badly burned. They begged for water and food, and Furgeson thumbed them to the rear under guard.

"This could be easy," said Furgeson.

Rader answered dourly: "Sir, nothing comes easy."

As if to punctuate his comment, a first outburst of automatic fire came at First Platoon's line in the creek bed, and its people went flat.

"That's surprising," said Furgeson.

"Not as surprising," said Rader, "as that they put us in a third time."

"I guess," said Furgeson, "that's our job." Though he said it, it was clear that he really didn't feel that way. Housley, acting as the artillery FO with First Platoon, was trying to get the measure of the resistance. At first, it seemed nothing much to worry about, a rather mild swarm of badly aimed bullets. The men had hit the dirt more from weariness than sudden fear. They were well in line where a bend in the creek was furnished with the hamlet's banana grove. The grove afforded a little shade. The men would pick up and get moving again in a few minutes with no help from the guns; such was Housley's judgment.

The thought was no sooner born than it was exploded by the fire of a heavy machine gun ranging in on the line from the same ground whence had come the opening AK-47 fire.

Housley jumped to the RT and gave his direction to the support battery: "Left three hundred, drop one hundred."

No sooner had he given the correction than he heard a voice cutting in on his "freak" (frequency) and saying in perfect English: "Correction, right four hundred."

Housley yelled: "No, left three hundred, drop one hundred."

The other voice said: "Correction, right four hundred."

The battery complied.

Housley cried out: "What the hell is going on here?"

For five minutes the battery went with the mystery voice, and so doing, it shelled a column of First Cavalry troopers who were descending the ridge to the northward.

Then Housley got it: The mystery voice was a Charlie who understood artillery.

Still, knowing the problem, Housley had no solution. His every attempt to straighten things out with the battery was foiled by the mystery voice, which cut in and scrambled the message. At last Housley gave it up, and repeated over and over: "Cease all fires."

Two thump gunners tried to knock out the machine gun. No

luck. It was either beyond effective range or too solidly emplaced. The gun kept firing and the men stayed down.

Pardick, from his position two hundred meters to the rear, had been listening in on radio to this baffling exchange. Nothing seemed to make sense any more. "All of our people seem to be going crazy with the heat," Pardick told himself.

It was no idle thought. Around Housley, the platoon began to melt away, not from the enemy gun, but from the fire of the high afternoon sun. The machine-gun crew, PFC's Reddy, Schmitting, and Stevens, keeled over together, one, two, three, domino fashion, and were dragged rearward, unconscious. Five minutes later, Lieutenant Hill collapsed. Within the next hour (which takes us up to 1530) nine more men had passed out and had been evacuated rearward.

One thump gunner, little McCorkle, who had missed his Charlie on opening day, was still going strong. He had found a snug position on a trail in the banana grove, from which he felt he could get a better line on the .51 machine gun. A small hut stood directly to his rear. He squatted there on the trail pouring out grenades from his launcher. More than a dozen riflemen came up and grouped around him.

McCorkle's one-man stand was suspended only when he saw a Soviet-made RPG-7 rocket coming straight toward his head. In a split second he flattened and the rocket exploded into the hut behind him. Housley, who had gone flat and closed his eyes, looked up astonished to see McCorkle still alive.

He said: "Your head's still on; I can't believe it."

McCorkle answered: "I'm not sure till I shake it."

Both were shaking all over and laughing at the same time. They snapped out of this touch of near-hysteria when word came from Furgeson that the platoon should swing left out of the creek bed.

Heiner moved out first, lugging an M-60, so that he could

throw out a covering fire while the platoon was making its right wheel.

His mates saw him stagger forward, make about twenty meters, and pitch over headfirst. They thought he had been hit by a bullet, but the sun had done it again.

It was now 110 degrees in the shade.

The author spent this same afternoon at Plummer's position, about one-half mile from where Furgeson was fighting and can attest that the outing was no picnic.

PFC's Smith and Erlenbaugh crawled forward to look Heiner over and see what was wrong. The examination over, they picked him up and lugged him off. Halfway back to the ground where Rader was regulating operations, they both pitched over from heat prostration. For minutes the three lay flattened in the sun, no one giving them attention.

When Heiner dropped, Housley passed his M-60 to one of the replacements (unidentified) who had come from Tuy Hoa that morning, saying: "That's yours. Get it going and keep it that way." The unknown took over the machine gun.

PFC Housley, like PFC Comazzi, was mastering the whole art of command in one day. They are figures at whom to marvel.

There were now just thirteen men left of what had been a platoon. Housley, by default and through strength of character, had become the moral leader. He sent one squad of seven men up the left bank in an attempt to outflank the .51 gun. Being that kind of soldier, he went along. They worked through the banana grove and entered a thick copse of bamboo, which proved so resistant that they swung back to the path on the edge of the bank.

Housley heard Roberts yell: "Grenade!" He had seen a head and an arm suddenly rise up from behind a pile of gravel next the creek.

All eight men hit the deck together. The explosion drove

shards into the right arm, neck, and back of PFC Harold Motley. A second grenade went far over the flattened column. The third grenade landed between Roberts and PFC's Tony Giolando and Robert Johnson. This third bomb was a dud.

Encouraged by that brief interlude, six of the eight Americans grenaded into the stream bed, aiming for the bank of gravel. More grenades came sailing in on them. They arose and ran back the way they had come, all that is but Giolando, who had to take it slowly because he was supporting Motley. The running was a mistake; it was no afternoon for running.

Aid Man Amaya promptly toppled over from heat prostration. The others, breathless, shortly reported what had happened. The report had a strange effect on PFC Russell Palm, until then a non-activist. He grabbed four frags, advanced over the same path taken by the patrol to where he saw the dud grenade lying in the open, faced the gravel bank, and bombed it. Then he made a second trip of the same kind—the distance was about forty meters —to return unscathed and a little boastful. "I think I killed that .51 gun," he said. "I saw something big blow above the bank."

There was no time to think that over. Immediately, the Charlies came on down the creek bed in strength, grenading as they advanced. It was a bizarre performance, heralded by the mooing and bellowing of about twelve cows that the Congs were herding down the creek to serve as their buffer and shield. The Congs were right in among the cattle, keeping all that beef between them and the bank, where the Americans at first sat reacting not at all, just plain puzzled by the spectacle.

McCorkle was the first man out of his trance. He yelled: "We gotta kill all those cows; get with it!" and began firing his M-79. Roberts, Giolando, Krebbs, Calvert, and Housley grenaded as fast as they could throw.

Shortly, the creek bed was an abattoir and the water ran crimson, some of it colored by the blood of men.

PFC Robert Johnson, the platoon RTO, was playing Gunga

Din, always on the move from the hamlet well to this small fire line, keeping it supplied with water. That the line survived at all was due to his care. The enemy AT gunner must have been watching him through glasses. He took Johnson under fire on one return journey and got off five rounds trying to stop him. All five were narrow misses. As Johnson arrived laughing, Calvert was saying to the other men: "We better gather up our gear and move back; we're not doing any good around here."

McCorkle said: "What ain't worth doing ain't worth doing well; I heard it somewhere."

The new kid whom Housley had turned into a machine gunner one hour before stayed behind to cover their withdrawal with fire. He was perfectly willing; in fact, he had volunteered.

In less than a minute, Calvert and his party of eleven breathed more easily, and figured it was time for the kid to fall back on them. He had lost them to sight behind a hedgerow, and with the solid bank protecting them they huddled briefly in the field, while Calvert weighed whether he should send someone back to get the gunner.

An RPG-7 rocket landed right among them, exploded heavily, and the blast flung them about like so many rag dolls. Housley was kicked ten feet, landed on his back, and at first it felt as if it were broken: he had come down on his own PRC-25. Calvert was wedged in the hedge and crying: "Medic! Medic!" Both of his legs were bleeding badly.

PFC Richard Krebbs picked himself up from the ground, but stayed half doubled up.

Giolando asked him: "You hurt, Krebbs?"

Krebbs replied: "My back pains a little."

Then he pitched forward on his face; one shard from the rocket had punctured his lung. Perhaps he was lucky at that. His upper body had been wrapped around with six loaded ammunition belts, and instead of exploding the shells had cushioned the blow.

Giolando was bleeding from slugs that had hit him in the back and arm. Johnson was wounded in the leg. Only Roberts was unhurt.

Housley ripped away Calvert's trousers to see what could be done for him. Both legs had been clouted hard. The left leg seemed to be in the worse shape.

Calvert kept saying: "My God, this pain is killing me; I can't stand it. It's terrible."

Housley could not understand all the fuss. There were two long cuts on the leg, but these were merely deep flesh wounds. What escaped his eye was that a large slug of metal had gone through the sole of Calvert's foot, ripped upward through the flesh and shattered the ankle bone.

Assisted by Spec 4 Bob Moore, the company's chief RTO, Housley carried Calvert rearward to the casualty collection point. As he turned the sergeant over to the medics, Housley became aware that he had forgotten his radio and left it in the field. He returned to look for it, but the PRC was missing; someone had picked it up. While he searched briefly along the hedgerow, another rocket exploded within twenty meters of him. He started back over the trail, and alongside it found the missing radio. Though a hole had been drilled right through the outer shell, the machine still worked. That delighted him. But as he studied the punctured PRC-25, a great light dawned. That slug could only have come out one way; it had to be somewhere in his own back. He put his hand to the small of his back and the fingers came away very sticky. So he had been wounded after all. Though he had stayed unaware of the hurt to his flesh, the slug would win him his first Purple Heart.

Except for Waterboy Johnson and the unknown kid who had been left on the machine gun, First Platoon was now wholly wiped out.

Lieutenant Colonel Wasco and Colonel Hal Moore, whose

Brigade had taken over the operation for First Cavalry Division, had flown into Furgeson's CP about noontime. The visit had been short, and nothing had gone off very well.

After Furgeson had briefed his two bosses on the situation, Moore, who was sometimes called by his troops "Old Yellow Hair," which had been Custer's nickname, came forth with a wisecrack: "Looks like you're opposed by about one rifle squad."

It was exactly the wrong thing to say.

Furgeson replied: "Sir, it's the toughest fucking rifle squad you or I ever went against."

Moore said: "Get your men moving."

Furgeson replied: "Roger."

And that was about it. Moore was never a soldier noted for tact in dealing with people beneath him.

Furgeson said to Sergeant Lonnie Thomas, "Have the guys move on."

So even as First Platoon had slogged to its fate in the creek bed, holding down the right flank in virtual isolation, Third Platoon had deployed on the extreme left; this put Second Platoon in the center, walking straight toward the same houses and hedges where it had been belted and bloodied the day before.

For forty meters Second Platoon sailed right along, feeling no pain, keeping pace with the rolling barrage. The men passed the big barn and filed through the gap in the hedgerow. As they fanned out once again to form a line, Charlie lowered the boom. It was AT fire and machine-gun fire, coming at them at a sharp angle from off their right flank, accurate and unrelenting.

Everybody hit the dirt.

Sergeant Bob Woods yelled: "I'm shot; got it right in the ass." The bullet had drilled both cheeks.

PFC Tom Robinson was flattened by a bullet through his right shoulder even as he was diving for cover.

A machine gunner, PFC Bruce A. Masters, had his trigger

finger shot off. He wrapped the stump in a handkerchief and worked the trigger with his big finger. Then, being something of an exhibitionist, he took a running leap at the hedge, almost landing on the back of Private Wilson, the psychologist. Masters waggled the bloody stump in front of Wilson's nose, yelled "Look at that million dollar wound!" jumped back over the hedge again, and resumed firing the machine gun.

Colonel Moore had stayed on to witness the move to contact. But Furgeson had walked away from him, which was perhaps just as well. The captain had posted himself with the Third Platoon, which, separated by one hedgerow from Second, was enjoying a fairly quiet afternoon, a stone's throw from the hot spot.

Mixed with the automatic fire, Second Platoon was now drawing occasional rifle rounds from its direct front.

The cry: "Snipers! Snipers!" arose.

PFC Albert Goodenart, otherwise inconspicuous through the day, simply studied the situation and did some figuring. Some of the fire from frontward seemed to be plunging; other bullets came in flat and cut a straight groove through the grass and dirt. There had to be at least two snipers. One was under the haystack in the center, and the other was firing from the large tree just beyond it.

Goodenart talked over his conclusions with Sergeant Lonnie Thomas, who said: "I'll go for the guy in the haystack."

He did it in a dash, whipped out a pack of matches and set fire to the hay, then ran back to the hedge.

Right on his heels came Goodenart, waving his rifle, grinning from ear to ear, and shouting: "I shot the sonofabitch out of the tree."

While the hay still blazed, Thomas moved his men forward about thirty meters beyond the stacks. Third came up even with Second in the other field. It had not yet drawn any fire. This move was completed by about 1430.

Furgeson expected nothing but a negative holding operation thereafter. Second Platoon had moved on beyond the line of sight of the AT gun crew and the machine gunner. The company was waiting for the column from First Cavalry Division to come on down the ridge finger to the north and join it in the hamlet, pinching out such resistance as remained. This was the agreed-upon maneuver. Furgeson continued to pop smoke grenades for the cavalrymen to guide on.

The ARA came on, four ships altogether, and with Furgeson directing them the gunners laid on an east-to-west strike rocketing the ground forward of the company line to soften up the positions before the cavalry arrived.

Almost an hour passed with nothing else happening to the two platoons, who remained in ignorance of First Platoon's ordeal. After a time some of the men became careless and began bunching. Furgeson threw out more smoke, this time well over to the right of Second Platoon, as a target marker for another strike, this by an oncoming pair of Sky Raiders.

That's when the lightning hit Second Platoon in the form of an 81-mm mortar stonk; the salvos came on, three rounds at a time. The first salvo merely stalled and startled Second Platoon, the closest explosion being twenty meters off. The second salvo wounded Sergeant Jack Lanksford and PFC James Coffee, both getting it in the right shoulder. Coffee ran for the rear to summon first aid. Other men picked up as if to follow him. Lanksford stood there yelling: "Take it easy! Take it easy! Don't run!"

If good advice, it was badly timed, there being no possibility of taking anything easy. The thing had been very close to panic.

PFC James Stokes was shot down, one bullet in his left arm, another in his left leg. PFC Ezell Dickson took a bullet through his back as he turned toward the hedge exit and the big barn. Most of the men of Second Platoon were now either looking or drifting that way.

PFC Jim Liddell started walking out, leaving his helmet where he had rested during the hour-long quiet. He yelled out: "Hell, I got to get my pot!" turned about, and made a running dive for it. An 81-mm. round landed dead on him and blew him to pieces.

Now everyone was moving back. PFC Nate Hall, a few paces ahead of the others, made a running dive to get over the hedge. The jump killed him. As he landed on the far side, an 81 round came down on his back and detonated; little was left of him.

The shells kept coming as men scrambled for cover behind the hedges and buildings. Within the next ninety seconds—before they could make it to safety—seventeen more men of Second Platoon had been wounded and were through for the day.

That left only Comazzi, the one man to escape the stonk that otherwise destroyed the platoon. So for this one day Second Platoon came almost exactly even with First Platoon, and it was too foundered to have any thought of clearing its own casualties. The men were down and spent and only Comazzi was moving. In First Platoon only two able-bodied soldiers remained.

Furgeson, who was still in the field, called on the RT to Third Platoon: "Forget everything else. Swing over this way and start moving these casualties."

Platoon Sergeant Martinez got his men moving. Then he called Furgeson: "I'm all alone here now, holding this field with one machine gun. Do you think I'd better move back?"

Furgeson said: "Stay right where you are; hold the position."

Said Martinez: "Roger."

Another new lieutenant, John Dorsey, had landed from Tuy Hoa just in time to help Sergeant Rader organize the evacuation of the casualties. Rader thought he was right on top of the mission; standing with Dorsey on the same ground where he had cleared the wounded that morning, he signaled the medevac Huey to come in. The pilot mistook the signal, came down in a field right next to enemy country, paid for his mistake by taking a dozen or so bullets through his frame, and took off; he flew toward Rader with the bullet stream still following him, decided he'd had enough of such nonsense, and hightailed it back to Tuy Hoa.

Dorsey directed the lift party to carry the wounded men into the banana grove. They would have to wait awhile and it would be cooler there.

Furgeson had seen six khaki-clad NVA soldiers pop up from behind the perpendicular hedgerow while the machine gun was blistering the Huey; two of them were firing AK-47's in the same direction. A third was firing an RPD, a light machine gun. From where they stood, they had Furgeson and all others still in the field in enfilade, but paid them no attention.

Furgeson fired his M-16 and saw his bullets chop down the gunner.

PFC Snyder got a second Charlie as the NVA soldier switched his AK-47 to aim at Furgeson.

The other four disappeared.

The indestructible Housley, his Purple Heart wound stanched by a bandage, had again come forward, just in time to draw one more mission. With Housley were PFC Roger Haseltine, the company's RTO link with battalion, PFC Moore, and Spec 4 Edwards.

Furgeson said to Housley: "There are two bodies out in that field. Go get them."

The four worked their way halfway along the parallel hedgerow. There Haseltine came across two packs and a rifle and turned rearward with them. The other three continued forward and at last came to the bodies. As Moore started to slip a poncho under the body farthest forward, a light machine gun opened fire right down the hedgerow. Edwards, Moore, and Housley ducked lower and kept at their work, Housley struggling to get a poncho under the second body.

Moore started dragging the first body away. Housley half knelt. Two mortar rounds exploded right between them. Housley was blown backward and knocked breathless as he crashed the bank of the hedgerow. He saw Moore fly through the air, then pass from view as he fell on the other side of the hedgerow. Edwards, who had lagged behind, had disappeared from the scene.

Housley arose shaking. Not a fragment had touched him, though he was dazed from concussion and the collision with the bank. Moore crawled back through the hedge, miraculously still whole of skin, but no less rocked than Housley.

Housley said: "I'm too pooped to drag anything out of this field except myself."

They crawled back to Furgeson who was on the far side of the big barn. Edwards and Haseltine were already there.

Furgeson asked: "Where are the bodies?"

Housley said: "Sir, I couldn't bring them out."

Furgeson said: "You turn around, go right back there, and get them."

Unaware, Furgeson was asking far too much of two men.

The four started back.

From behind the hedge, Comazzi had watched the failure of Housley's mission. Now, taking PFC Henderson with him, he crawled along the hedge bent on extracting the bodies.

Henderson couldn't take the reek and the sight of the brayed flesh. He vomited and kept retching until Comazzi sent him back. Comazzi pulled each body a short distance, became exhausted, and gave up the struggle. The ordeal was completed by Housley and his three-man detail.

By 1730 the company, or what was left of it, was practically disengaged and the cavalry had not yet put in an appearance. Furgeson continued to get the message: "We will be there in one hour." The hour was long drawn.

Yet Barney Broughton's cavalrymen had not been dogging it on their attack downward from the crown of Hill 258.

Just as with Plummer's company moving at right angles from

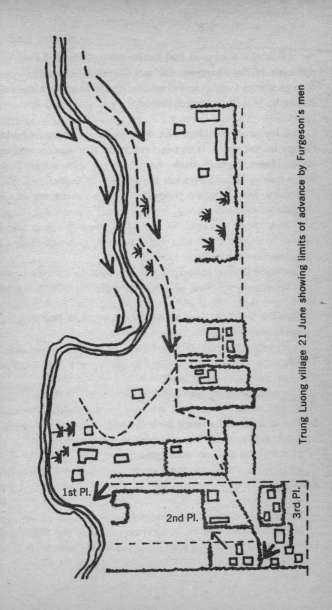

Trung Luong village 21 June showing limits of advance by Furgeson's men

1st Pl.

2nd Pl.

3rd Pl.

them toward the sugarloaf, their morning enemy had been nature, the terrible heat of the sun, the tortuously slow going through the rock slabs and brush, the frequent rests to stave off exhaustion, the too-early draining of the canteens.

Otherwise the movement itself seemed to make tactical sense in the terms of Fort Benning. Pointed as they were, Charley Company, 2/7, under Captain Lyman C. Duryea, Jr., and his attachment, Lieutenant Robert J. Fullerton, of the 11th Pathfinders, were the other side of the pincers. With Furgeson held fast by the enemy front at Trung Luong, the cavalrymen should be able to debouch on the NVA rear and rip through. That's how they hoped it would be during the three hours in which they were descending to the flat of the valley, though their advance was beyond concealment.

The cavalrymen's arrival on the low ground coincided with high noon and the start of heavy engagement with a hidden NVA force that resisted until early evening. Two medevac ships managed to fly off the casualties—ten KIA and twenty-one WIA—but got bullet-riddled during the lift-off.

About two hours before that happened, Furgeson had called Wasco to say: "My company is no longer combat effective; I request permission to withdraw."

Here was both truth and reason.

Wasco replied: "Permission denied; you stay where you are." It was an answer that did him little credit, but he was getting news of the cavalrymen's plight and Furgeson wasn't.

The NVA monitored this transmission, and reckoning that Alpha Company was no longer worth worrying about, gave undivided attention to the stalling of Charley Company of the Seventh.

Medevac ships continued coming into Furgeson's ground. By 1800 all the KIA's and the critical cases among the WIA's had been flown out, which almost coincided with Duryea's clearing of his casualties.

The fighting ended as the last of the NVA blew the whistle and vanished. When finally at about 2000, the cavalrymen entered the hamlet, there were only forty-two men around Furgeson. All others were dead or down.

On the other hand, Duryea's company still had a fair body count, 143 men, and since no one said a word about their fight, Furgeson too easily took it for granted that they had slogged along all day virtually unopposed. The thought irked him.

Duryea asked him: "What are your instructions?"

Furgeson said: "I have been told that I would stay here through the night."

Duryea shook him off, saying: "I don't like this position; I don't like the way this fight smells; there's something wrong about it; I wouldn't stay close to this village for anything."

There was a moment of truth; some instinct warned Duryea that there was an X factor in the situation eluding both of them.

"I wish I'd kept away from it," said Furgeson, "but it's too late now. By the way, may I lead you to a lovely piece of high ground? It ought to be plenty big for both of us."

So it was back to the ridge finger for the third time. The move by Furgeson's forty-two battered soldiers, begun at 2100, wasn't completed until after midnight.

They had to tote all the extra loads dropped by the hundred or so men lost that day. They got no help from the cavalry. Though that griped the paratroopers, they didn't grouse out loud about it. A few of them were able to sack in shortly after the witching hour when churchyards yawn. The rest had to stand guard duty and LP duty around the perimeter, sharing it with the cavalry. They didn't like that, either. The Screaming Eagles had given full battle that day. They all assumed the cavalrymen had merely taken a walk in the sun. Furgeson felt browned off about it, but didn't argue. He was too beat down.

Next morning Furgeson was told by Wasco that his outfit would have to spend the day making a sweep westward toward

Dong Tre. It was no longer a company; it was hardly a platoon. But they did what they were told and they spent 22 June scrambling over the heat-baked ridges, encountering nothing that was worth fighting except the inordinate difficulties imposed by geography and the burning sun. They were content that it was so and that the opportunity to fire did not arise.

In two days, exclusive of heat casualties, this company had lost fifty-four men. Few, if any, United States rifle companies in the Vietnam War were more sorely tried.

By way of contrast, the Second Battalion of the Seventh Cavalry, under Lieutenant Colonel Herman L. Wirth of Union Beach, New Jersey, was lifted into Dong Tre out of An Khe on the following morning.

Baker Company took position outposting the small hills to the north that had given Captain Holmes such a bad first night. The rest of the battalion marked time until late afternoon.

Then came the report that one platoon from the First of the Ninth and the Recon Platoon from the First of the Eighth were pinned down by intense enemy fire just five thousand meters to the northwest of Dong Tre and needed help.

What was said about the fire was true enough. There had come about a chance meeting engagement between this reinforced patrol and an NVA patrol. The toll of Americans was five dead and three walking wounded. Since the news smelled of attack from a new direction, Wirth's battalion was mounted and rushed to the fire scene. From two hundred feet above I saw them dash out to form their perimeters as the choppers lifted just prior to sunset. Their motions indicated that they were fighting fit and full of beans.

This battalion was in the field five days threshing about and poking into odd corners. It was bounced about on strike after strike. Not once did it hear a shot fired or even see anyone who looked like a Charlie. Hopping all over the map, it achieved nothing except a view of new scenery, none of it inspiring, this being a particularly drab region of Vietnam. Having wasted time and boot soles in a wholly futile exercise, the battalion was withdrawn on 28 June, its troopers not more sunburned than disgusted with the war.

By then other Americans were probing about in Trung Luong hamlet to destroy its stores and otherwise discourage its future use as a garrison point.

At first they found little that was startling. Then, on that same day, one ancient who had stayed in the village said to a Vietnamese interpreter: "Come with me and I will show you something interesting."

It was a dishpan in a field, the rims of the pan set even with the earth; the basin was full of dirt, so the pan stayed hidden. Removal of the dishpan disclosed a deep shaft below. The discovery led to some rather extensive exploring by specialists among the American engineers.

Too late, it was learned that Trung Luong was served by one of the most extensive tunnel systems anywhere in the country. Of this came the enemy mobility that had cost Furgeson so many of his soldiers. The NVA had been moving through the catacomb to get from one firing point to another. Without this tunnel system, the air and the artillery might have broken the resistance, but the heaviest bomb could not cut through to the tunnels. Furgeson had made all the right moves, yet none had worked out in the right way.

On 5 September 1966, an NVA précis of the operation fell into American hands. It was marked "kin," meaning confidential. The paper reads as follows:

This time, against the Americans, we have killed 800 men. We suffered heavy losses, 200 KIA and many MIA. We failed to enlarge on our victory by not strengthening our forces. There was no water and no rice for two days.

On 21 June at night (in the tunnel) the command committee and the party cell met to discuss withdrawal from the battlefield. The cells of Comrades Cuong and Hao said that they had wiped out an entire enemy infantry company. Son, a soldier, took advantage of his malaria to remain behind. We found him with an enemy leaflet in his pocket. He is no longer with us.

Violations of policies: Cadre and some soldiers stole sugar. Comrades Son, Tan and Nga became too anxious because there was no rice. Comrades Vi and Vo Dinh Tu got too excited in combat, exposed themselves and got hit.

During the [Trung Luong] operation we killed 144 enemy soldiers and we downed five aircraft. The corpse of one comrade-in-arms was eaten by dogs and pigs. We must take more care with pigs. The discipline, working manner and physical conduct of our troops leaves much to be desired.

We must tie prisoners up after capture, throw them down into the pit and then carry them away in hammocks. One hundred percent of our party members are heroic. They substituted bananas and rice gruel for real food for five days. They have glory, pride and confidence. Though deprived of food and forced to substitute wine for water, the 41st Group was successful. Some men of Group Minh Luong would not believe we had killed altogether more than one thousand of our enemies.

Here was not spectacularly extravagant claiming and bombast by the military in Hanoi. It was normal and fairly representative of the way in which the war was misrepresented to North Vietnam's soldiers by their own leaders.

Given a propaganda opening through which any thinking person could drive a ten-ton truck, the government in Washington took no advantage of it. Nothing was done to circularize corrective information, to the American people or to the NVA soldier who entered South Vietnam believing that everything was coming his way. He stayed duped till the last.

There is no explaining this failure on our part, though it is possible that all who should have been concerned were too busy with other things.

As with all else in this peculiar war there was a Humpty-Dumptyish inability to distinguish between the important and the unimportant. This lack of perspective—the chronic fault of acting without first getting the ducks in line—was mainly at the highest political level in Washington, the White House with its coterie of crisis managers and the Office of the Secretary of Defense, which is not to say that the military commanders were in all things prescient, prompt, and positive.

PLUMS TO
PLUMMER

Nothing in the campaign is more difficult to put in a sensible light than all the beating-about on Hill 258. Whether Colonel Moore's preoccupation with the big ridge had a sound tactical basis is the primary question. The enemy could not use this piece of high ground to dominate Trung Luong Valley; it helped him only as a lure and ambush site for one-time use only. There were many other available landing areas, the countryside being quite open. Otherwise the ridge top had no important operational utility, and the Charlies had not contested its possession out of any belief that it would sway the battle one way or the other. They had set up there simply to kill as many Americans as possible. But professional officers do get overly preoccupied with high ground simply because it is high. I have found this failing in any number of them.

Mack and his worn men proceeded once again to prowl the rimrock before being lifted out to lick their wounds in Tuy Hoa. (Mack, a very brave soldier, was later KIA.) That they would find nothing of consequence was almost a foregone conclusion. For the enemy to have returned to the crest, under full observation in full daylight, would have been impossible.

Plummer & Company were also slowed in getting away, partly because canteens had run dry, and Plummer was reluctant to start the march to the sugarloaf hill without water. His hesitations were calculated, rather than emotional. The day was excruciatingly hot and the air atop the mountain was lifeless. The water did not come, however, and at 1100 on 21 June the company began the descent, moving out in platoon columns. There was a brief holdup near the top of the slope when Sergeant Odom, beating through a clump of bushes just because he was curious, found an enemy machine gun and two cases of ammunition.

Halfway down the ridge, having moved not more than about a thousand meters, the company ground to an enforced halt. Several things were going wrong at one time, as is usually the case when a rifle unit gets flummoxed. Though they had been clambering downgrade on a steep slope for most of the way, four men had already been prostrated by the heat. Plummer knew that to attempt to carry them along would deck more of his soldiers. So he would wait on the slope for the medevac Huey. It would take some time. Plummer saw no reason to rush, and in so feeling, beyond question he was right.

Then too, some of Lieutenant Whelan's people were in a running fire fight just to the north of the river, and bullets from this small affair (it seems incredible at that range) were glancing off the rocks around Plummer & Company. No one seemed anxious to run risks with this friendly fallout. Though Plummer threw out smoke to stop the fire, the company ground to a stop pretty much on its own and Plummer decided it was time for lunch. A few hands broke out rations. Most of them were too much athirst to eat. Still, sitting was good.

The long wait under the noon sun had such a dizzying effect that the command was hardly under control when it started downward again and it definitely was not moving as one body.

Plummer sensed the involuntary and unexpected dispersion but was himself so flummoxed by the heat that he made no move to arrest it.

One platoon stayed right on line, heading by the shortest distance for the sugarloaf. Another platoon veered to the right and westward under the impression that a bend in the river lying that way was the nearest watering point. A third platoon swung obliquely to the left on a line halfway between the river and Trung Luong hamlet because its leader thought he saw some Americans moving in that direction.

Plummer watched the fan-out and did nothing. There was nothing to do. They were already spread out of control. Men crazed by heat are no more responsible than men high on dope.

No hurt came of this accidental, unauthorized way of going. Group by group, at widely separated intervals, the off-flank elements straggled back to get with Plummer again. The company was solid when he first talked to Lieutenant Woods at the base of the sugarloaf, and Woods miffed him by inviting his people to drink of a stream flavored with dead men. It was then about 1500.

Of these wholly unmilitary meanderings could have come an unintended deception and Plummer, though at first chagrined by his loss of control, tried to put the best possible face on it. He said to Woods: "If the enemy had his eye on the valley, he could not possibly guess that you have been reinforced by a full rifle company, the way we dribbled in here." .

The lieutenant didn't answer; he hadn't watched the approach. Plummer had found Woods in his CP—a pup tent pitched on a sandbar in the river trench. Colonel Broughton had already advised Plummer that Bravo Company would bivouac around the sugarloaf that night as "visitors or guests of the 327th." Plummer so told Woods, who gave him a much too brief rundown on what his own men had been through. Because Woods had spoken too modestly, Plummer's soldiers stayed pretty much in contempt of Woods's people thereafter. Or perhaps their attitude could be blamed on troop nature: "We are always the best, which makes you not so good." There should have been a warm embrace; the fact is there was none. Plummer as the new arrival might have changed this, but Plummer had to be himself.

The NVA bodies from the slaughter by Woods's men stank to high heaven. They still lay there within the banana grove under a broiling sun. Oddly enough, the smell did not tell Plummer that the Screaming Eagles had been through a somewhat more than meager skirmish.

After establishing his CP at the northern base of the sugarloaf, so that he would be in the long shade cast by the bamboo screen along the river bank, Captain Plummer next seated his 81-mm. mortar battery on line with the command post on his side of the river within a rod or so of his own tent. That put quite a few eggs in one basket. He then climbed to the top of the sugarloaf to view the position all around for the first time.

What he saw did not assure him. Despite its sheer banks, flat surface, and rectangle of ready-made foxholes, the sugarloaf did not strike Plummer as an ideal position for defense against an enemy that was lacking artillery; as to its exposure to intensive pounding by mortars, he was right beyond question. (These initial qualms Plummer discussed frankly with me as we sat on the sugarloaf hill the following day while the area was still under random rifle fire from the distance.) About why Plummer discounted the truly significant and advantageous features of the ground at first glance, there is only the explanation that he was still dizzy from the heat. A commander in that condition is less than half able to appraise his problems.

Two of his platoons had already taken position atop the sugarloaf hill, mainly because Woods still had one of his platoons idling in the foxholes and Plummer's lieutenants had decided that it was sensible to flesh out the circle. A third Bravo platoon deployed to the northern quadrant of the perimeter, across the river and facing the rice paddies. The Fourth Platoon was split into two flank watch forces to tie-in the northern quad-

Foxhole circle

Bamboo screen

The creek

Plummer's perfect hill, seen from the north

rant with the position on the hill. The critical weakness in these dispositions was that, if the NVA attacked due westward out of Trung Luong hamlet and up the river trench, the company CP and the mortars would be hit first. Plummer was aware that he was fully exposed to a thrust from that direction but accepted the risk, reckoning that from where he sat he could move more readily to any threatened quarter. And besides, that was the only way he could get the CP set up in the shade of the bamboo screen.

The early evening was quiet. At 1900, Plummer got word over the RT from Colonel Broughton that he should take command of the whole force. Still, he talked it over with Woods and they agreed to act in tandem, a right friendly arrangement.

At 2100 the position as a whole came under a desultory small arms, machine-gun, and mortar fire, with a few rifle grenades also hitting the top of the sugarloaf. The enemy mortars had to be emplaced somewhere to the south and the fires seemed to be unobserved, as no adjustments were made. Four-fifths of the rifle grenades proved to be duds. The added danger was just enough to make men nervous and keep them wakeful.

During these same hours on 21 June, Charley Company of Broughton's battalion, Eighth Cavalry, as has been told earlier, was closing on Furgeson's company in the position next Trung Luong village. There was enough fire breaking on and around the sugarloaf so that the distant sounds of the action to the eastward made little or no impression on the people in perimeter next to the river. They had been told nothing about what was happening to friendly forces just around the corner from where they lay and they felt no curiosity about it. The two forces were as detached from one another as teams playing in different ball parks.

To the left of the CP and approximately twenty-five meters up the river, Spec 4 Allen Wright, a twenty-one-year-old Negro from

Philadelphia, was leading a fire team that outguarded the flank.

One of his riflemen whispered to him: "Al, there's more noise coming out of those bushes than seems natural."

Wright whispered back: "I think you got something," and emptied a clip from his M-16 into the clump.

One prolonged piercing scream came at them out of the dark. "We got something," said Wright.

Then a round dozen potato masher grenades sailed in on their ground all at once.

They went flat on their bellies.

Every grenade dudded out.

Emboldened by their luck, Wright and two others rushed the bushes. They found an AK-47 rifle and a pack, and leading upstream, one blood trail. That was all.

At 2300 a light mortar round exploded just outside of Plummer's CP. PFC N. W. Radke was slightly wounded in the left leg. One shard cut into the head of Sergeant George Clark, so wounding him that he lost his power of speech. Though muted, he refused to quit the fight. Clark kept moving around the position, his head beating like a drum.

Their part of the valley stayed well flood-lighted most of the time. The 105 howitzer battery at the crossroads was putting up illuminating shells every few minutes and at 2230, the flare ship, Smokey the Bear, came on to provide more light, staying until 0200 when a shortage of fuel compelled a withdrawal.

By then the valley was graveyard quiet. Still, almost no one slept. The men were ouchy and apprehensive and Plummer was feeling a restiveness that forbade relaxation and was reflected in his actions.

At 0500, he called Lieutenant William Hughes on the RT to say: "Give your people a wildcat." By this he meant that all hands in First Platoon should be brought to full alert.

At 0530 he called all other platoon leaders and gave the order: "Everybody wildcats."

There had been no suspicious sights or sounds. For hours, not one shot had been fired.

At 0535, Plummer gave another order to all platoons over the RT: "Everybody ready for a mad minute at 0545."

He thus indicated that upon his signal there would be a full firing with all weapons to last sixty seconds, just in case there might be a few Charlies skulking about.

At precisely 0543, the sugarloaf and the near ground exploded with fire as the NVA suddenly laid it on with AK-47's, mortars, machine guns, grenades, and rockets, all at one time.

Two minutes early, Plummer called over the RT: "Let it go now. Give it to 'em. Mad minute. Everybody firing. They'll be charging us."

All platoons were set to comply. Plummer's was probably the luckiest alert in the Vietnam War. He was wearing horseshoes—horseshoes all the way.

Plummer stepped from the tent to look about.

He could see mortar flashes to north of the river and hear many chanting voices much closer by. He put up his red flare signal for the mad minute to reinforce his oral order and to speed reaction. And as he did so he grinned, well knowing that things were coming his way on his lucky, lucky day.

PFC Robert G. Barnes, twenty-three, of Erieville, Pennsylvania, was Plummer's RTO. This highly original character was having his first time in combat. A wrestler in the heavyweight class, curly-haired, and a great jollier, Barnes had been drafted after dropping out of Nebraska University.

The noise now wakened Barnes, who was dozing next to the CP. He sat up and said for anybody to hear: "This can't be real; nothing comes on anyone that fast."

He felt his brisket curling up around his throat. The mad minute had shaken him to the marrow.

The other RTO, PFC Arthur S. Mayer, had slept through everything.

Barnes shook him by the shoulder and said: "I think we're being attacked."

Mayer answered: "Forget it. We're making all that noise."

One minute passed.

Barnes spoke again: "I'm telling you, that's the Charlies firing."

Mayer spoke with sudden respect: "You're right, my friend, that's them."

Sergeant First Class Winfield S. Bledsoe, at thirty-five, with nineteen years in the Regular Army, was the company old-timer. He had been wide awake. Even as the attack started, this son of Huron, Ohio, could hear the swish of the enemy mortar rounds leaving the tube.

Looking in the direction of Hill 258, Bledsoe could see flashes off-and-on about halfway to the base of the hill. Guessing the range at 450 meters, he got the unit's 81-mm. mortars going. In twenty minutes he had fired off everything he had and thereafter kept the battery operating for a time by dipping into the 327th's stores without first asking permission.

PFC Steve Guash interrupted Bledsoe at his work to raise a question: "Hey, Sarge, what in hell is going on around here?"

Bledsoe answered: "It's a mad minute."

The kid asked: "How can a minute last an hour?"

Bledsoe said very soberly: "Son, we're under attack; don't you get it?"

Said Guash: "No, I don't get it at all," and strayed away from the position.

Bledsoe said after him: "You must be playing this out of a Boy Scout manual."

But Guash was gone from earshot. Here was a soldier who simply could not believe that he was in a fight. With little variation, such incidents have been recorded of Americans brought under fire at Bastogne, Kwajalein, and Pork Chop Hill.

On the left flank and upstream, where earlier Spec 4 Wright had made his foray, machine-gun and rifle fire dusted the half-squad outposted there. The enemy weapons were based not more than thirty meters to their immediate left somewhere along the bank. So thick was the bamboo growth that the Americans could get no fix on the position. Yet the same growth helped shield them. The company was using no LP's, so designated, Plummer believing their use here was a sure way to get men killed, because of the sinuous course of the river trench on either flank. That was how he explained it though his reasoning was not exactly clairsentient. Instead of LP's that might fire and fall back or risk being overrun to illuminate the enemy attack in silhouette, he had instructed his men in the far-out positions to rely on defense with claymore mines. Spec 4 Wright remembered that instruction. He tried to fire his claymore to take the heat off the position. Nothing happened. Charlie had already slipped in and cut the wire. The discovery made Wright feel very lonely.

Looking in the direction of the bush overgrown area to his right and north of the river, Wright could see North Vietnamese soldiers, khaki-clad, milling about. Though the night was now pitch black, these enemy figures stood clear in the light of the flares fired by the 105 battery at the crossroads. They were within easy range. Wright thought about that and decided it was not his night to dare the lightning.

Then suddenly his attention was diverted. From upstream, not more than seventy meters away, or twice the distance at which the NVA were capering, there came a great mooing and bellowing. It was the first notice served on Wright or anyone else in his outfit that, somewhere beyond the banana grove, a cattle corral was still going strong, the presence of which the 327th's moppers-up had somehow overlooked. There is nothing in the book instructing a lone Spec 4 on watch duty what is to be reported about the comings and goings of cows.

The khaki-clad figures crossed the river to Wright's side and tried to get the cattle out of the corrals and headed toward Wright's piece of the perimeter. Confusion. The drovers couldn't drive and the Communist stock would not cooperate. Horns down, the animals veered outward and rearward to right and left and there was no stopping them. The spectacle fascinated Wright, as it did Sergeant Clark who had come up behind him. Their United States Army basic training had not taught them that war could be like this. While they looked on, the last of the cattle vanished into the dark, leaving the line of khaki-clad drovers in the clear. Wright fired, a couple of NVA soldiers dropped, and the others disappeared.

A crackling sound right at hand, almost as his elbow, drew his gaze toward the river. The muzzle of an NVA rifle was being pushed through the screen of bamboo lining the south bank; the metal was within a few feet of his head. He fired a burst from the M-16, heard the man scream, and then heard the splash as the body fell back into the stream, leaving the gun and a pack on the bank.

Two NVA soldiers had somehow filtered through Plummer's lines north of the river and had gotten across the stream. They clawed their way up the front face of the sugarloaf and were mounting the crest when a frag grenade exploded in their faces and blew them back downslope so that they died next to Plummer's CP.

An NVA mortar could be seen; that is, its flash was plainly visible, as it fired from Hill 68, a knoll about three hundred meters off, to the right front of the perimeter and north of the river. The company mortar section under Sergeant Bledsoe put six 81-mm. rounds on the knoll and the tube fired no more.

Over the RT, Plummer got the word from Lieutenant Robert Heath, commanding Third Platoon, which held down the northwest corner of the sugarloaf where 327th's soldiers had beaten back the charge out of the banana grove: "I need help bad; give me what you can."

Sergeant Odom was up there. The fire from the west out of

the banana grove was again beating men down, such was its intensity. Some of 327th's people, facing this fire for the second time, had lost heart and moved out to the rear of the sugarloaf, leaving a thirty-meter gap in the foxhole line. Heath was side-slipping some of nis soldiers from the northeast corner to fill in, but reckoned that he couldn't stretch the full distance. One M-60 had been left behind when the 327th group pulled out.

Plummer ordered three squads out of First Platoon to get with the fight on the sugarloaf. Odom shifted himself to the hot corner, and marked the signs of flight. Packs and hand weapons were scattered about. Seven of 327th's wounded had been left behind, men hit by the volleying that had routed the others.

Odom got on the RT to Plummer: "We have casualties. Get medics and stretchers to the front of the sugarloaf. We'll move them that far."

Bledsoe was not the only hand sweating out an ammo shortage problem. PFC Tommy C. Nettles, a twenty-year-old Kentuckian, was dispatched from the hill by Odom to rustle machine-gun ammunition wherever he could find it. Nettles, who has a very marked stammer, headed straight for Lieutenant Woods's stores on the bank of the river next the CP.

To First Sergeant William Branch of the 327th he said: "I—need—some—machine—gun—ammo."

He reached for the case.

Branch replied: "Boy, you can't have it; that's my ammo."

Nettles hoisted the case to his shoulder, said to Branch: "Then —you—go—fight—the—sonsofbitches," and took off.

Then he turned and looked back, just long enough to say: "I—will—see—you—later—much—obliged."

Ten minutes later he was back, and reaching for a second box. Branch asked, "Where are you going, boy?"

Nettles: "Taking—this—with—me—just—watch—me."

This time he went out carrying the ammo case on his head.

Five times he made the journey, each time to cut into the stores Branch was charged with guarding, each time to hear Branch protest and in the end do nothing about it.

Odom was already fitting his own men into the foxholes on the northwest corner, and he was just in time.

The dawn was coming fast. Odom could see now for the first time that a few NVA skirmishers were already inside the position atop the hill. Some were crawling about, scrounging equipment. Others had settled into the foxholes. More were crawling up the bank.

Spec 4 Leroy Williams, a twenty-one-year-old Negro from Tampa, dealt with four of them. One stood above a foxhole, firing down into it, but still missing a wounded 327th soldier who huddled there. Leroy shot the Charlie through the back, killing him instantly. The dead man fell atop the wounded man from the 327th.

Another Charlie was in the act of picking up an M-16. Williams fired at him and missed. PFC Elmorro Wren of Memphis ran for him, grappled with him, and tried to wrest the weapon away. As they tussled, the Charlie still clutching the weapon, they lost balance and together pitched over the western embankment, rolling together to the bottom. The Vietnamese was holding onto the weapon. Wren broke loose; he kicked the Vietnamese into unconsciousness, grabbed the rifle, unpinned a grenade, put it under the body, then raced back up the hill, yelling: "I got it; I got it." For this exploit Wren was awarded the Silver Star.

Williams then shot two more skirmishers as they came crawling up the embankment.

So went the attack and its repulse. Odom and Staff Sergeant Mario Rodriguez spent their time crawling from foxhole to foxhole, distributing grenades. The riflemen stayed in their foxholes or prone shelters, rolling grenades down the slope or throwing them when they saw a group target amid the banana palms. Though the few Charlies within the position had been liquidated, the skirmishers kept coming on from the banana grove for another quarter of an hour.

Daylight by then was fairly full. The flank positions which had been set to block access via the stream bed were now held only by a few men of First Platoon and they were feeling the pressure.

Over the RT, Lieutenant William D. Hughes of Cordele, Georgia, called in to Plummer: "We're getting a lot of fire, more grenades than anything else. They're lobbing them into us from the bank."

Suddenly, the pressure against the sugarloaf began to subside. The NVA had pulled out of the banana grove, leaving behind some wounded, to renew the attack from the far side of the palms, employing machine guns and rockets.

Plummer got a call from Third Platoon's RTO, PFC Wren.

Said Wren: "You better send first aid. We need help real bad."

Plummer had the senior medic, Spec 5 Arrellano, right at hand. Because Hughes's earlier message had seemed equally urgent, Plummer sent Arrellano first to the position of Spec 4 Allen M. Wright, who was covering the left flank upstream from the CP.

Arrellano was back in a few minutes, saying: "They don't need me there; nobody's been hit."

Arrellano then headed for the sugarloaf. The hour was about 0630.

Before Arrellano could report to the sugarloaf, Lieutenant Robert P. Heath was on the radio talking to Plummer.

He said: "This may be hard to believe but we don't have a single casualty. The only wounded up here are the seven friendlys from 327th and we have moved them to the front of the hill."

Plummer said: "You must be crazy; a battle can't go that way."

Arrellano set to work treating the 327th wounded in just about the same minute when the NVA started dusting the top of the sugarloaf with bullet fire and rockets. Arrellano acted as if it weren't happening, though all other hands jumped for the foxholes. For continuing first aid under fire he was awarded the Silver Star.

Plummer was trying to talk to 2/327th on the RT. He wanted medevac and in a hurry; several of the battalion's wounded were in grave condition. But he couldn't raise 2/327th. There was too much traffic on the net. One forward observer was busy calling for support fires from the artillery and ARA. The FAC was also asking for one thing or another. So was Colonel Moore. He tried and tried again to get his requests through, then gave it up, saying: "Hell, this is plain babel."

By 0700, the pressure was off, so far as the western face of the tabletop was concerned, and Odom and Wright were throwing out smoke to provide guidelines for the oncoming ARA. An enemy mortar battery from somewhere in the rear of the sugarloaf zeroed-in on the smoke and kept hammering away.

Plummer kept putting it to his subordinates over the RT: "Please tell me what's happening."

Wright reported: "The VC is coming to me down the stream bed, along the bamboo screen, and across the paddies to the north. Our people can see them from the tabletop. They're calling to me. No enemy is getting closer than thirty meters."

Wren said: "From here I can see no less than fifteen bodies in the banana grove. The VC is trying to carry them out right now."

Corporal Willie Sims, with Third Platoon, was acting as artillery recon NCO. Sims was from A Battery, 2/19th. He called for fire from the two batteries at the crossroads, brought it as far on the eastern side of the sugarloaf as the buckwheat field, lifted it over the hill, then dropped it on the banana grove and held it there to stampede the enemy evacuation parties. Odom and Wright saw the VC drop the bodies and run.

At 0800 Bravo Company lost its first man. PFC Richard Washington was hit by a mortar shard in the right ear; it was not a deep wound but it so impaired his hearing that he had to be shipped home.

Coincidentally, an air strike came in. Phantoms hit off both flanks of the sugarloaf with napalm, CBU's, and bombs, and got in so close that some of the metal was dropping into the American position.

The FAC who was with the strike put it to Plummer over the radio: "Left Tackle, this is Top Sail Gulf. Do you know that you are number one target for strikes in Vietnam today?"

Said Plummer: "I am not enjoying the honor."

Said Top Sail Gulf: "Roger. Over. What else do you need down there, Left Tackle?"

Said Plummer: "A chance to use this RT for something more important."

Plummer was still trying to get through to 2/327th and that outfit was trying to get through to him, with neither having any luck. It was most exasperating.

One Charlie, his face and the side of his body smoking from napalm, came running into the CP area, from beyond Wright's position. No one tried to stop him. He had a broad grin on his face when he lay down to let the aid men work him over. He never quit grinning, at which the Americans marveled.

Another lone Charlie charged through the banana grove and started up the sugarloaf. A thump gunner grenaded him at a range of twenty meters. The missile, failing to arm, hit him in the chest and flipped him over in a somersault. He arose and scuttled away in the direction whence he had come.

Odom yelled: "Did you ever see anything like that?"

Colonel Moore was now overhead in his command ship and was asking Plummer: "What's your sitrep?"

Plummer said: "I can't give you one. We're under attack but I really don't know what's happening."

Next he was talking to the battalion commander, who was

asking the same question from up there somewhere in the sky

Said Plummer: "Under attack. Holding our own, I think. Will keep you informed if anything happens."

Calls were coming in from the platoon RTO's. Everyone was running short of ammunition. Especially lacking were grenades and M-79 rounds.

Plummer asked: "How do we start? We don't have much left here."

He got on radio to Broughton, saying: "We gotta have ammo resupply, and send along some C rations."

The RTO, Barnes, spoke up: "I've got nine hundred M-16 rounds on my back. You can have them all if you just let me have the RT."

Barnes, the most over-loaded man in the company, hadn't fired a shot and was getting a little tired of it all.

It was just about then—at 0900—that the enemy came on in his final gasp of the day.

Something less than a charge, and bigger than a forlorn and futile try, a body of about sixty NVA, having given up the approach through the banana palms, attacked against the southwest corner of the sugarloaf.

No signal of any kind had preceded them. They came on well bunched and at a slow lope, not determinedly, but stumbling, and they did not yell or make any sound as they advanced. It was as if they already knew that they would be ground small. In the forefront was a lieutenant waving a pistol.

They got within thirty meters of the rear slope. Overseeing the southwest corner was an M-60 machine gun, the same weapon that the 327th had abandoned when all of the crew became wounded. Feeding the gun now were PFC Roosevelt Madison, Jr., of St. Louis, Missouri, and PFC Dennis M. Spahn. A cousin of All-Star pitcher Warren Spahn, young Spahn would later be killed in action.

Now he was to have his big moment. On one side of the

machine gunners was Spec 4 John B. Veal and on the other, Spec 4 Peter Mills, both riflemen. Firing together, these four men smashed the charge with perfectly aimed fire that continued till the enemy fled.

The enemy mortars were still pasting the hill. While four men were beating down half a company, PFC's George Jones and D. T. Vincent were hit in the upper body by pieces of shell, though neither was gravely wounded. At the same time an ARA rocket pod caught fire, was dropped from its chopper, landed dead center on the sugarloaf hill, and failed to explode.

Plummer was now sweating hard.

Over the RT he asked Colonel Moore, who was still orbiting overhead: "I'd like permission to use tear gas."

Moore replied: "I'll let you know."

Moore had to ask permission, also, and besides there was no good reason to believe that tear gas, or any other gas, would be useful in this situation.

Hughes came to the CP—it was about 0930—to say: "I believe our situation is becoming critical; we just don't have the ammo."

Shortly afterward, Lieutenant Woods of 327th, shirtless and looking very much worn down, came calling to say: "We've tried, and we can't get Charlie to pull back from in front of the position [that part of the perimeter that lay north of the river]. I would like you to think about giving up the hill and leaving it to the enemy."

Plummer asked, "Well, are you worrying about whether you can hold where you are?"

Woods said, "No, I believe we can hold it."

Still not knowing that 327th people were no longer engaged in the fight for the sugarloaf, Plummer replied, "That ought to answer your question."

Then for a few minutes they wrangled about whether it would be best to smite the enemy southwest of the sugarloaf with napalm or let him have it with tear gas.

Woods said, "I say no to tear gas; my men have no masks."

Plummer replied, "That's tough; we'll use it."

A more amusing argument than this would be hard to find. With both officers the premise was that Woods had a say because he still had some people on the hill, which was wholly contrary to fact. So the tiff was altogether pointless. In the end Colonel Moore decided against the use of napalm, then passed the word to Plummer that he could use tear gas, after which Plummer concluded that the wind was in the wrong direction for tear gas anyway.

About 0940, Lieutenant Whelan, who had continued to guard the northern face of the perimeter, called Plummer to report: "There's a VC platoon three hundred meters away, moving in this direction, between me and Hill 257."

Plummer called in another air strike.

Resupply ships by this time were landing in the buckwheat field to the east of the sugarloaf. With Sergeant J. J. Johnson playing honcho to the operation, Second Platoon's people were choggying the ammo, water, rations, and medical supply around the perimeter. Lieutenant John W. Langston, Bravo Company XO, who normally stayed with the trains, had flown in with the supply choppers.

Even as he reported, Plummer received a message over the RT from an observer aloft: "Large body of enemy moving through abandoned village directly to your west."

When the information was relayed to Corporal Sims, he very seriously put the question to Lieutenant Michael C. Livengood, the artillery FO: "Don't you think it's about time we blew that village off the map?"

Livengood told him to go ahead.

Sims's TOT was delivered just where wanted; quickly the village was ablaze. From his place on the sugarloaf Odom could see a few NVA who had survived crawling southeastward along the hedgerows. On his suggestion, Sims switched the shellfire to the line they were taking.

Barnes, the wrestler-turned-RTO, was getting ouchy.

He said to Plummer: "I been sitting here all day, running this damned machine and not firing a shot. How about giving me a man's mission?"

Plummer said: "OK, you asked for it. Go forth and bring me one of their uniforms, and I'd also like two weapons. Get that many and you can have one."

Barnes jumped to it, and set up his own patrol. Taking two men with him and sticking close to the bamboo screen south of the river, he moved out about 150 meters to the westward.

Suddenly, he heard a bolt click right next to his ear. Within the bamboo, almost at his elbow, stood a wounded NVA soldier. For a split second they glared at one another eye to eye. Then PFC Robert W. Forshaw emptied a clip into the Charlie's chest. He fell next to a partly concealed antitank gun, his hand still clutching his AK-47.

Barnes started to paw the two weapons. "The big one if for the boss," he said, and then bowing very elaborately to Forshaw, he added, "the little one if for you."

Ten minutes later, he was back with Plummer, saluting him and saying: "Sir, mission accomplished."

By then, Colonel Moore had dropped in for a call. Along with him was a large party of PIO's and correspondents from Dong Tre.

Colonel Wasco, commander of the battalion from the 327th, was already on the ground and talking to Woods.

Plummer looked the delegation over, sniffed a bit, and said aloud: "I guess this means things are dying down more than a little."

At the south end of the sugarloaf where First Platoon's men still crouched low unconvinced that the fire fight was over,

Spec 4 Tom Lambert was rubbing his eyes, not believing what he saw. For more than an hour a dead NVA lieutenant had lain to Lambert's right, a few feet away, even with the foxhole line. Now, incredibly, the body was inching down the rear slope so slowly that the motion was barely perceptible. In one hand the "corpse" clutched a light machine gun, in the other a pistol.

Lambert made a great leap through the air and pinned the body. Together they rolled down the embankment. The lieutenant, shot through the shoulder, wounded in both legs, and with most of his penis shot away, still fought back and had to be dragged kicking and screaming up the hill. Even when Lambert got him to the top, he would not subside. So Lambert picked him up several times and dropped him hard on the ground, yelling: "Damn you, stay still; you've got to have medical care." The lieutenant at last got the point: He was not going to be killed. Then he quieted down. While the aid men worked over him, he said: "We wanted to quit but didn't know how."

Two of the 327th's soldiers, acting on their own, had foolishly entered the banana grove scouting for enemy weapons. Word came to Plummer that they were pinned down by fire several hundred meters to the westward. He sent forth a patrol. It was too late. Halfway to the scene, one badly wounded man came crawling to them. He said that his comrade had died from a coup de grace bullet through the head. He himself had played dead and lived to tell about it.

About one hour later, from the northwest corner of the banana grove, Plummer & Company began the final mop-up with the NBC camera and crew following along. Second Platoon was doing most of the work. It was then just before noon.

On the sweep they took four NVA prisoners, including one captain. Three of the prisoners were wounded and had to be carried out in ponchos. The NVA captain had taken the precaution to write in chalk on the front of his jacket the word OFFICER. He spoke pretty fair English. His first words were: "Give me water and then I'll talk." Thus came about the first identification of the enemy regiment that General Norton had believed was somewhere eighty kilometers to the westward. Twenty-seven enemy dead lay under the banana palms. West of the grove Plummer and his group made their most startling find—nine dead NVA women soldiers, all bearing arms, the bodies clad in khaki, the close-cropped hair almost hidden by berets. In a nearby hooch, nine pigtails hung in a row, possibly for use on ceremonial occasions.

At the edge of the banana grove was a bamboo thicket and underneath this thicket had been excavated an eight-by-eight headquarters, equipped with chairs, table, and messing facilities. Beyond this find was a smoldering pile of hay. When the hay was scattered by Plummer's soldiers, another score of bodies was revealed. Many bamboo stretchers were scattered about. Apparently the hay had been set afire in the hope of concealing NVA losses. The body count to the westward continued through this day and the next, becoming 79 by nightfall, standing at 134 "certains" by close of the second day of search, 23 June.

Soon after the preliminary mop-up, a large crowd of Vietnamese women and children entered Plummer's lines, coming from hamlets to the west. During the fighting they had stayed underground in the tunnels and were little the worse for wear. All carried bedding, cooking utensils, or other household goods on their backs. They asked for evacuation and were flown to Tuy Hoa that afternoon.

Their exodus prompted Plummer to make a sweep of the west-lying hamlets. This sweep brought in another 110 civilians, not a few of them wounded. Several died within Plummer's lines before they could be flown to hospital.

The remainder of Broughton's battalion was brought to the sugarloaf position that afternoon. Alpha Company was sent on a combat assault to the west to try to regain contact with whatever was left of the enemy force that had engaged along the river. It was a vain hope. Alpha Company closed on the hill late that evening, having found nothing.

Plummer knew then that he had misread the enemy withdrawal. The survivors of Seventh Battalion, 18-B NVA Regiment had slipped away to the south. Two days later an enemy rallier confirmed this. He also said: "We thought we were fighting an understrength United States company. So we put two companies in the assault and held one in ambush."

PFC William D. Saunders was the final casualty of the fading fight. That afternoon he was wielding a spade, preparing to bury one of the enemy dead. He reached down to move the body a bit. A booby-trap grenade had been fixed to the waist. Saunders saw it and jumped just in time.

A shard the size of a dime pinked him in the right cheek. It drew so little blood that the wound was dressed with a Band-aid.

"That," said Saunders, "is worth a Purple Heart."

It was.

THE CAULDRON

PLUMMER'S FIGHT ON the sugarloaf won swift renown, not only because the press camp at Dong Tre was panting for a hot story, but also as the result of statistics.

After his two day mop-up of the environs, Plummer could claim that Bravo Company, without the death of a single man, had an honest body count of the enemy far greater than its own numbers. Though the boast was not idle, and had some basis in fact, there was no earthly possibility of determining how many of the North Vietnamese along the river and within the banana grove had been destroyed by the fire of Woods's people.

Fate simply willed it that though a company of Screaming Eagles for two days took the shock blows on this ground, the cavalrymen harvested most of the credit for knocking off the greater part of one enemy battalion. *C'est la guerre.*

As to how things stood on 23 June, while Broughton's battalion still tarried at the sugarloaf, the enemy presence in Trung Luong village, having evaporated following the withdrawal of Furgeson's company, the question in all minds was: "Where has that fellow Charlie gone?"

The captains and sergeants who only hours earlier had been fighting him in the valley on such hand-to-hand terms that there seemed little or no chance he could wiggle away were not more baffled than General Jack Norton who was reading through all the G2 poop that had any bearing on the subject. All that was certain was that Charlie was gone, and that, though he had slipped off in broad daylight, the Americans had done no maneuvering to close off fairly obvious escape routes when the fight began to flag. The conditions of the fight leave little room for doubt that this was within their possibilities.

The Second Battalion of the Seventh Cavalry, under Lieutenant Colonel Bob Lytle, having landed at Dong Tre on the night of 22–23 June, marched forth to try and pick up the scent. Somewhere around noon on 24 June, Lytle reported that he was in contact with an "enemy battalion" holding forth at a village, coordinates 959-666.

Of such slender threads, or vague reports, operations get going again in the Vietnam War. North of the village about two klicks lay fairly open country, well ridged but not heavily vegetated. Bringing the enemy to a fight where there is room for maneuver and little limit on observation is almost invariably a tempting prospect in irregular warfare; when he is opposed by highly mobile forces with an utmost advantage in heavy weapon power, it should not be his cup of tea. Of that may come a tendency to strike at once while the iron is hot, and when plans are laid on hastily, eventualities are seldom considered carefully.

This assault was indeed rushed. It was decided to throw in Broughton's battalion to the north of the target village to serve as a blocking force. Box the enemy in first so that this time he cannot eel his way out; such was the general idea. It came to pass in very late afternoon.

There was also another element, the lift. The 229th Aviation Battalion had spent most of the early afternoon picking up the worn-down pieces of Wasco's battalion that remained in the field and flying them back to Tuy Hoa. There had been "little contact," which is to say that the Hueys in this extraction were not much harassed by enemy ground fire. Still, it had been chore enough because of the same relentless sun that scorched men, ships, and earth throughout Operation Nathan Hale.

Bravo Company of the Aviation Battalion had been called first to LZ Eagle, the buckwheat field next the sugarloaf hill, where Broughton's people were readying for movement to the plateau north of Trung Thanh. It lay about five klicks to the southwest. At 1645, Charley Company of the Aviation Battalion, having completed moving the 327th's warriors back to Tuy Hoa, was in the process of refueling when word came from the battalion S3, Major William Johnson, that Charley Company should get up to LZ Eagle just as quickly as possible.

Major Willard Bennett, the company commander, took twelve Hueys and set forth. One of his platoon commanders who figures in the story is Captain Bobby L. Moore of Lubbock, Texas. The co-pilot on Bennett's Huey was Major Howard M. Williams of Elloree, South Carolina.

Another observer of much that followed was Captain Richard L. Lincoln, from Delta Company, a son of Billerica, Massachusetts. Four gunships from that unit were on another escort duty when in the late afternoon came instructions that they were to drop it, proceed to LZ Eagle, and from there ride shotgun for the slicks that would lift an assault force from that spot to a place called LZ Apple. Lincoln was one of the pilots. He knew nothing else of the operation except that the gunships should not use their rockets for prepping the LZ. There was some difficulty in the target area that made preparatory fires undesirable. It all sounded slightly vague.

Here was a quick mix for a quick fix. At LZ Eagle, one rifle commander, Plummer, was blasting away because he had not yet received his operations order. Though the heat of the day seemed no less formidable than before, the sun was low in the west and the bride and groom were as yet unwed. Yet both

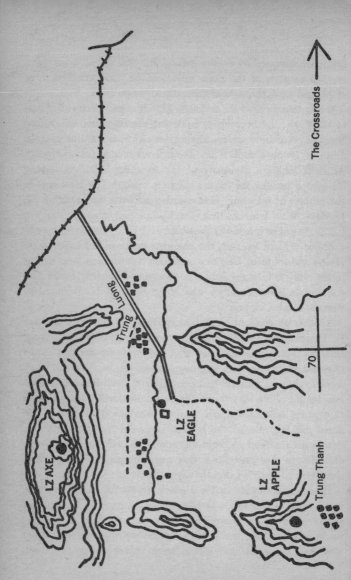

The Key Landing Zones in Operation Nathan Hale

parties to the contract—cavalry and carriers—kept the rendezvous and went through the motions of proper precaution.

The mission had sounded simple enough to the cavalrymen when it was first given to Charley Company's skipper, Captain Warren G. Boyett, twenty-five, of Jacksonville and educated at the University of Florida. Tending not to overcomplicate problems, Boyett's mind never strays very far from tactical brass tacks.

The battalion's mission was to attack the village of Trung Thanh, which lay about two thousand meters to the south of LZ Apple. The troops would be lifted that far, that is, to LZ Apple.

A Viet Cong battalion, the 80th main force, was supposed to be penned in Trung Thanh.

Charley Company was to secure the LZ.

That done, Plummer's Bravo Company would land on LZ Apple and at once strike south for the village.

If Plummer's luck was running, as it had been on Hill 258 and later at the sugarloaf, where only four of his soldiers had been nicked in two days of fighting, the main risks of the day would be dared by Boyett's people in running interference for Plummer on the landing zone. Or so it was reckoned.

With too little time remaining to ruminate on what might go wrong, Boyett and Plummer were flown out on a command chopper to reconnoiter from the air the ground where the two companies would set down.

The area proved to be high ground. Hardly a ridge, it was more like a small plateau set among ridges with a drop-off at one end. There was room enough atop the flat surface for five or six LZ's. One end of the plateau looked as if it were in torment from a fair-sized twister. Smoke and dust billowing from it rose high in the air. The artillery had worked it over and two air strikes had been laid on to soften up the ground for the landing. Therein lay the trouble: the prepping had been far overdone. Visibility on the designated LZ had been reduced to near zero, and if there happened to be any enemy force within seeing distance, that pillar of dust and smoke clearly signaled what was afoot. The punch was already telegraphed.

"When will they learn," asked Boyett, "that it is never wise to do more than is necessary?"

Yet neither to Boyett nor to Plummer did the conditions look prohibitive.

As they turned back to LZ Eagle, Major Willard Bennett (Preacher Six), the command pilot, said lugubriously: "I'm not buying that one. I'm sure the spot will never do. We will have to put down somewhere near it."

Though he did not say so, Bennett, during the reconnaissance, had already chosen the alternative bit of ground that would bear the name LZ Apple. Of that hunch came quite a payoff.

Less than one-half hour later Bennett and 125 of his men took off for LZ Apple riding in 22 slicks. Boyett, despite Bennett's forebodings, anticipated no real trouble and initially he had none.

The men got to earth unharmed and the aircraft lofted for the return to LZ Eagle without being fired upon.

Or rather, that is what Boyett thought had happened. He was so occupied with getting his men into position that he was almost oblivious to other sights and sounds.

The air crews had no such illusions. Fire from the ground had flamed and blistered them while they were making their turn-around.

Boyett was in slick No. 8. Its touch down was uneventful. The earlier arriving squads had dashed out to form the quadrant of the perimeter facing north toward the dust-laden area. If the VC had set up an ambush force, it would doubtless be there. By the time that the half-circle in that direction was complete and Boyett had accounted for all of his men, bullets and hand grenades were biting into the ground around the men of Third Platoon who had been the first to deploy.

The reason why things happened this way, with Charley Company making a soft entry, though the Congs were in position on the plateau, is perfectly clear. The enemy had set his trap around the dust-laden area, and needed time to redeploy and traverse the 250 meters of ground between the marked and the actual landing zone. This boded bad news for everything that would follow, though Boyett, as yet not putting two and two together, felt no alarm about what might come later. He knew only that for the time his men were fairly secure, the enemy bullets seemed to be coming from afar, and the number of hand grenades was so few as to be only a minor nuisance. Apart from the hedgerows and pieces of worn-down paddy banks, there were a few accidents of ground, mainly earth hummocks, to afford troops rude cover. Boyett's riflemen had hopped to it immediately. Most of them had flattened behind the hedge banks and were now firing to the north though they as yet saw no targets.

Still back at LZ Eagle was Boyett's XO, Lieutenant Patrick M. Griner of Altoona, Pennsylvania. He had been assigned to a chopper that was bringing along 81-mm. mortar ammo, sling-loaded. That chopper was not to move out until LZ Apple was secure beyond doubt. And that would be a long, long time.

Fifteen minutes after Boyett landed, the battalion CO, Lieutenant Colonel Broughton, was asking him over the RT: "Do you think Left Tackle (Plummer & Company) should come along now?"

Boyett hesitated for a moment, then replied: "Yes, he should come—because I need him!"

Plummer had already been told by Colonel Brockton, the Brigade CO: "Be prepared to follow up C Company immediately."

But communications were not of the best that afternoon. Colonel Brockton, who had been orbiting above the area where Boyett went in, was not physically present at LZ Eagle. From someone at the battalion level (and later Plummer could not remember from whom) came the subsequent instruction: "Hold where you are with Bravo."

Plummer relaxed, but not for very long. The command Huey landed at LZ Eagle and Brockton came on the run to tell him: "Get on the lift freak [frequency] immediately. The choppers are inbound."

Thereafter it was rush, rush, rush to get the three rifle platoons, ninety men altogether, squared away so that not a moment would be lost in mounting up. There were too few slicks in the lift to accommodate Weapons Platoon, which would continue to sit at LZ Eagle.

So great was their rush that numerous things were left undone. Hardly were they airborne when Plummer's artillery RTO, PFC Richard A. Abbott, normally a very steady soldier, asked plaintively: "Can't we go back, Captain? I left my M-16 lying on the ground." Abbott, twenty-six, is from Rutland, Massachusetts, and would win several decorations in battles to come.

Plummer dismissed him with a too terse "Hell no." Plummer was getting a bit edgy.

The command Huey had taken off first. In order there followed the serials of Second, Third, and First Platoons. The first pilot of the command ship, Preacher Six, looked back over his shoulder and gestured vigorously toward Plummer with his right hand, thumb turned down.

Plummer, who was thinking of himself as a seasoned hand after his big do on the sugarloaf, was still so green at the game that he did not know what thumbs down meant and he didn't think to ask. The signal said that they were headed for a hot LZ. All that Boyett had experienced in his first fifteen minutes had not been passed along to Plummer, another slipup caused by the rush.

Of greater curiosity was Corporal Willie Sims, thirty-two, of Newberry, South Carolina. Working as an artillery FO out of A/2/19th and attached to Bravo Company, Willie was riding along with men from Third Platoon in the second serial. The pilot of the Huey at once turned to his passengers and gave them the thumbs down sign.

"What's he trying to say to us?" asked Willie.

A door gunner answered sourly: "How stupid can you get? That means we're headed for a hot LZ."

"Oh," said Willie, "is that bad?"

Bennett had done too good a job of keeping a secret. Pressing on his mind was that which Plummer did not know and was just as well kept from him—the cost to the lift of its first brush with LZ Apple.

The last pilot, Captain Lawrence Woods, had been killed, shot through the jugular just as the Huey was about to drop its passengers.

Saying nothing about it to the riflemen aboard, the co-pilot, Warrant Officer Phalgraph, had taken over the controls, completed the landing, and flown off.

Another pilot, Chief Warrent Officer Anderson, was out with a broken right hip, shattered by a bullet that had come up through the slot in his seat. Two of the Hueys were limping back with no certainty of making LZ Eagle. By Bennett's recokoning, what had been hot on the first round would be a cauldron on the second.

Aboard the command ship, Bennett buzzed Plummer on the intercom to ask him: "Are you certain it is absolutely necessary to take these troops into that LZ?"

Plummer, not being able to read Bennett's thoughts and still ignorant of what the signal had meant, said: "Certainly, why do you ask?"

Major Williams, the other pilot, listened to the exchange, but was so busy flying the aircraft that he neither joined the conversation nor gave it a second thought. It's the mark of the warrior, this preoccupation with duty to the exclusion of worry. There is no other easement for combat stress.

Still in the lead, the command Huey, piloted by Preacher Six arrived above the plateau at just about dusk, with visibility fast going, circled the whole area once at two thousand feet altitude then straightened out for the approach.

Plummer could see the fire flashes in the field below. Next he felt fire, although at first it was not truly heavy. The chopper got to thirty feet above ground level. A bullet hit the door frame between Plummer and Preacher Six, glanced off, went between Plummer's arm and his belly, hit the armored seat, bounced again, and exited via the far door.

In Willie Sims's chopper, which was lead-off for Third Platoon's serial, the pilot circled the plateau twice, while ground fire gradually thickened around the Huey.

Two bullets popped through the floor next where Willie sat. Willie said nothing.

The pilot sheered off and led the serial back to LZ Eagle, to think things over and take a fresh reading on the situation. That is how it happened that Third Platoon came in late and put down without difficulty on uncontested ground well to the east of LZ Apple, which was one of the wiser actions of the evening. To all of this reasoning, Sims was oblivious.

In the end, only one man of the three platoons failed on his own to keep the appointment. That was PFC Otis Saddleblanket an Oklahoma Cherokee. Otis later explained that when the time to jump out came his gear had become so entangled with the webbed fittings of the Huey that he was bound to his seat.

The command chopper continued its forward rush just a few feet above ground and Plummer along with the others went for earth in a flying leap. It was a neck-breaking try, and though no necks were broken, every man lost balance and pitched head-first into the dirt, afterward to arise badly scattered, scratched, bruised, and shaken.

The rotors were raising such a dust storm that the men could not see one another. Plummer, on his feet again and limping

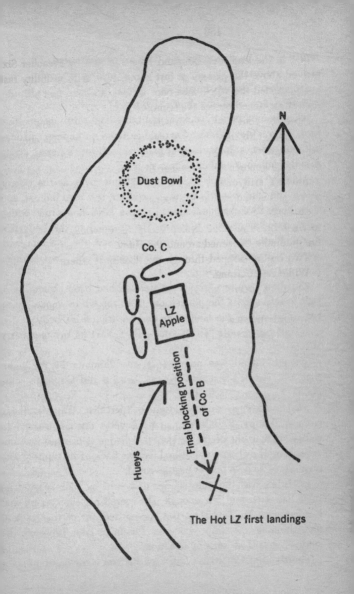

N

Dust Bowl

Co. C

LZ
Apple

Final blocking position
of Co. B

Hueys

The Hot LZ first landings

forward, glimpsed through the dust a few skirmishers lying flat in line and firing.

He called: "Boyett! Boyett!"

A voice answered in a shout: "I'm here!"

Then he saw Boyett, standing not more than thirty meters from him. He was waving the troops into perimeter. Plummer's people without order, automatically responded to Boyett's signal, fitting into the gaps in the other company's line.

Another Huey came in, flying the same path as the others. While the craft was still twenty feet in air, one man fell out, and with body spread-eagled, landed atop a large hedgerow, which seemed to bounce him upward. He dropped to the hedgerow again. Plummer, flattened by this time, saw the incident with shock, not recognizing the victim as one of his own soldiers, Sergeant Leroy J. Christian.

Christian's white phosphorus grenade had been shaken loose by the fall, and as the pin fell out of it, the white smoke plume rose high, out of the hedgerow, and all around his body.

Boyett called out: "That's your guy; I don't let my men carry WP."

Though Boyett was numbed as was Plummer by the sight that was Boyett's first odd reaction. And it did Christian some good.

That workhorse among aid men, Specialist Army Arrellano from A Battery, 2/19th FA, heard Boyett's cry and rushed to pull Christian out of the smoke-filled hedge. Christian was unconscious. His chest was crushed and his back badly injured. The medic bent to help him as best he could.

Christian was the only soldier delivered by that Huey. The pilot had seen and felt enough. He veered his chopper off and headed back to Tuy Hoa. Getting no account of that bugout and thinking the ship was lost, Plummer later reported the soldiers aboard as "missing in action."

Shortly after Christian's fall, First Platoon came in, and on the decision of a wise pilot it was landed without injury several hundred meters off the LZ. That is, for the most part.

Lieutenant Hughes was in the lead Huey of First Platoon's serial and though this unit came in last and braved the thickest ground fire, there was no hesitation. Pilot after pilot tried to barrel straight in. Not all made it.

That ever-steady NCO, Sergeant Odom, rode in the chopper just behind Hughes. The ship neither touched down nor hovered. It was in motion a few feet above earth when Odom and his six men jumped clear. They had decked on the right side of the LZ. The time was about 1930 and it was too dark to see anything clearly.

Odom sprinted for an east-facing hedgerow, his men following along.

Settling them in behind the embankment, he told them: "Fire low, keep it on that next hedgerow." They were also told not to grenade unless grenades came in on them.

The squad was left very much alone. In landing, it had become separated from the rest of the platoon.

After twenty minutes of this, Odom thought he had better do some scouting; he felt no certainty that the squad's fire was doing any good. So he left Spec 4 Leroy Williams in charge and, hunched far over, ambled west.

The account of Odom's landing is as he gave it. The fire that boiled up around the Huey had not impressed him at all. There is this offsetting description from Leroy Williams: "Man, the fire came from both sides and there was so much of it that I figured we was trapped between foe and friend. Odom didn't know any more about that than we did. After we got set it was the same way, lots of fire and no one knowing where it comes from. Then Odom comes sliding along. And he can't tell, either."

The first person Odom ran into was Boyett.

Charley Company's skipper asked him: "Have they told you your boy has been hit?"

Odom's stepson, PFC Thomas A. Cook, was a rifleman in Boyett's company. He had beaten Odom to Vietnam by several months and was about to return to the United States for training as a chopper pilot.

"How bad is it?" asked Odom.

"Just a slight crease in the neck and nothing to worry about," was the reply.

Continuing in his search for Hughes, Odom at last found him on the far side of the LZ. Hughes had been scouting about looking for Odom.

Enemy fire from west of the LZ suddenly built up sharply. Both men flattened, then crawled to the friendly (defended) hedgerow to get a better look. Peering over the bank, they saw the bulk of a much larger hedgerow about thirty meters distant to the southwest. From their own hedge, another embankment zigzagged toward this main source of enemy fire. Cutting through that perpendicular hedge, halfway along, was a heavily parapeted military trench not more than fifteen meters away.

Hughes and Odom, the first men to understand it, realized with something of a shock that the alternate landing zone, so summarily chosen, was a well-prepared enemy military position.

It was a little late to do anything about it. The last of the Hueys were coming in and would put down within twenty-five meters or less of the enemy's main fire base.

Had these same works been manned when the first serials had come in during daylight, the LZ would have become a slaughter pen.

Sergeant Allen Wright rode the third from the last chopper. The pilot three times made his approach, and twice gave up the idea of landing because of the intensity of the fire. Each time he sheered off and returned to LZ Eagle. The plane had been badly overloaded and the pilot reckoned that any kind of hit would mean a crash. Wright had been given responsibility for the unloading of three five-gallon water cans. He saw during the

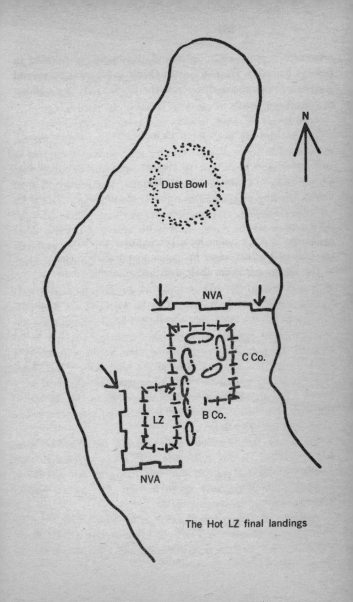

The Hot LZ final landings

first two passes that he couldn't possibly turn the trick. If he jettisoned the cans from above, that forty pounds of weight could crush somebody below. The chopper simply could not take the risk of tarrying while he carefully removed the burden.

He made up his mind: to hell with the water cans.

On its third try out of LZ Eagle the chopper dropped the squad on LZ Apple. Wright and his fire teammates sprinted in one direction; the rest of the squad went the opposite way. Wright came to a large hole in the ground, deep enough to cover a man standing and sized just right for the fire team. "This is for us," Wright yelled, and jumped into the hole followed by the others. They stayed there, right in the center of Charley Company's formation, and with that position they were perfectly content. Well before this, the enemy had dealt the American air assault its hardest blows of the evening.

In the next to the last chopper of the assault-in-main rode PFC Rodriguez, Staff Sergeant Charles M. Edwards, and PFC Tommy C. Nettles. Edwards was drilled fatally through the left chest when he jumped from the ship. Rodriguez took a bullet through the right knee at the same time Nettles was hit by a bullet in the jaw and the force of the blow popped his plates from his mouth so that he lost them in the dark. The teeth were found amid the dust in working condition on the following morning. The Huey, drilled by a dozen bullets, nevertheless lofted and got away unhurt.

The Huey had touched down outside the friendly lines. Rodriguez and Nettles still made it to cover under their own power, Nettles rubbing his jaw and trying to say something, possibly unprintable, very much in vain. The mouth worked away but the words wouldn't come.

Arrellano, the overworked medic and ex-Boilermaker, saying nothing to anyone, walked forth to bring in Sergeant Edwards. His comrades saw him next backing away from where he had picked up Edwards. The sergeant, now dying, was being supported with one arm. With his other arm, Arrellano was clutching an M-16 and pulling trigger as he retreated. Arrellano's rifle was shot out of his hand just as he reached the friendlys unhurt. Hollywood writers will never top that scene.

The pilot of the Huey that had dropped this load of grief was the Texan, Captain Bobby Moore. From his angle, it was a quite different story. He had heard Major Bennett sound the call to go in again, but had decided, after a 180-degree turn, to make his approach from the opposite direction.

Bennett told him: "In that case, at least wait until I've cleared the LZ," advice that any traffic cop would call elementary. So Moore continued his circling, meanwhile watching the four choppers operating directly under Bennett. They took so much fire that Moore changed his mind again. He would move still farther north for the approach. The other two ships in his platoon went first. Moore felt no deadly pressure until at two hundred feet fire came at him from both sides with such intensity from behind the hedgerows that the door gunners and the six riflemen aboard pressed trigger without letup as if bullets had gone out of style.

They got within two feet of the ground, the Huey still winging. Three riflemen jumped off on the left and rolled, head over heels. Edwards, Rodriguez, and Nettles tumbled off on the right and were immediately shot down. The Huey's right-door gunner, PFC Joe Kelly, saw these three get it, then as the chopper swerved, saw three flattened forms on the other flank, and yelled: "My God, everybody we had got hit!"

Moore strained at his harness to verify the bad news. But only for a second or two. There were too many bullets clouting the hull of the chopper to think long about that. He said to Kelly: "They can't all be hit; maybe none got hit."

Kelly knew better.

The climb had begun. Moore saw another chopper coming in about forty feet above him. He heard its pilot, CWO Donald Estes, yell: "Throw it into emergency."

About then, PFC Philip B. Waltz, RTO for First Platoon, called over to Hughes: "I see another American body out beyond our lines. May I bring it in?"

Hughes passed the buck along to Plummer on this one. Plummer replied: "Permission refused. Wait until I get a check on all of my people."

That would not be easy. All of the people were not yet in. The last chopper of the lift was just beginning its approach.

The four gunships from Delta Company that were doing escort duty between LZ Eagle and LZ Apple had used only their machine guns in protecting slicks and troops during the descent and deployment of Boyett's soldiers.

Not only did Captain Lincoln and the other pilots feel themselves restrained by the admonition heard while in flight that heavy fires would raise too much dust on the landing zone, but at first there seemed to be no real requirement for shock action. By the time the tag end of the first lift was getting raked by automatic fire, it was too late for the gunships to go in.

Then as Moore's flight came on in the second lift, the scene below fairly exploded with enemy fire. Lincoln could see from the tracers what the slicks were up against. On both sides, a line of trenches not more than 150 meters apart ran perpendicular to the landing zone. Both trenches were manned; the middle ground, where Boyett's men were deployed, and into which the Hueys were descending, was caught in a machine-gun cross fire.

Lincoln heard Captain Thomas Haskell of Columbia, South Carolina, call out: "We gotta get into this." The four gunships dropped to forty feet above ground, then made a racetrack pattern of their attack as they chugged round and round blasting the enemy trench lines with rockets. But for the supressive effect of their fires, a minor calamity might have become a disaster.

Lincoln saw one machine gun firing from a tree, high above the northern trench line; he could follow the tracer bullet stream clearly. On his next time around, he rocketed the tree and saw the gun and gunner blown clear. The last slick was just then making its run.

Lincoln's craft was now out of rockets, as were the other three gunships. They stayed on their tight circuit; the door gunners were working their weapons.

Haskell had had his hydraulics shot away.

He asked Lincoln: "May I have permission to return to Tuy Hoa?"

Lincoln said: "Go."

Spec 4 Eagen, Lincoln's crew chief, called out: "Look at that. Those Charlies are standing in the trenches and firing at us with rifles."

Three radios were going in Lincoln's aircraft.

Suddenly Lincoln heard several voices asking: "Where is White Four? Where is White Four?"

Lincoln heard someone answer: "You see that big ball of flame in front of you? That is White Four."

The voice was utterly flat as if the speaker were drained of all emotion.

White Four was CWO Don Estes, the pilot of the last Huey bringing in a remnant from Plummer's last rifle squad. Somewhere around a hundred feet above ground, a bullet had gone through the engine, killing it. That, at least, is the best educated guess about what happened.

Lincoln heard Estes scream three times: "Throw it in emergency!"

So did Bobby Moore, and that was all that ever came from

Estes. The ship kept straight on and vanished over the edge of the plateau three hundred meters to the north of where Estes should have touched down. The shock of the finish was missed by the flattened infantry line.

Moore, already sensing the worst, called to Major Bennett over the RT: "Axle Six, this is Axle White One. White Four just crashed off the end of the LZ."

Moore followed out, calling for Estes by name, but getting no answer. He saw the crashed ship just over the lip of the plateau; he dropped lower and started to circle above it to see if anyone survived. The ship exploded in a great ball of flame and Moore pulled off. In the Huey had perished four crewmen, the co-pilot Warrant Officer D. S. Townsend, the door gunner, Spec 4 L. P. Lebrun, and the crew chief, Sergeant W. E. Steier, and three of Plummer's fighters, Specs 4 Johnny Nickey and Adell A. Alston and Spec 5 Bobby J. James.

Moore headed for Tuy Hoa with three bullet holes in his aircraft and six in the only other Huey still flying from his platoon. Of the ten aircraft that Major Bennett had brought to the fight, only two were flyable by the following morning.

With the departure of the last Huey, the enemy seemed to lose all interest in continuing the fight. The reaction was as if the NVA had set up an ambush specifically to entrap aircraft and was set on avoiding any meaningful exchange of fires with infantry.

The fight began to cool by the time Bennett's ships were past the horizon.

Within an hour thereafter the top of the plateau was quiet except for occasional rifle shots in the distance from beyond the edge of the plateau.

Neither rifle company had fared badly after troops had deployed into firing positions along the hedgerows. Boyett's RTO, Spec 4 James Melton, got a bullet in his midriff and one of his friends, Spec 4 Gary T. Myers was hit by a bullet in the jaw.

Such were the only wounds in that unit. Some of Plummer's losses have already been described in detail.

Plummer was now checking around the perimeter to see what names needed to be added to the list. PFC Rudy Sandoval was down with grenade frags in his back. Corporal Richard H. Campos had taken a slug through the left cheek. Spec 4 Johnnie B. Veal, Jr., had been drilled by a bullet through the right shoulder. PFC Willie J. Bridges had several grenade frags in his right hand. Sergeant Leon Fletcher was wounded by frags in the right leg and arm, PFC David P. Hughes had taken several in the forehead, PFC Arthur C. Sutton had a badly shot-up right thigh, and PFC William D. Saunders had taken several shards in his right shoulder. Spec 4 James H. Milton was one of the few critical cases, with a bullet through his stomach.

It cost Plummer the better part of an hour merely to check out his casualties. So badly had the two companies become scrambled during the somewhat frantic landing that midnight had come and passed before men were properly sorted out, with all hands accounted for.

They stayed on the plateau that night after evacuating the casualties. Neither then nor later was there any advance on Trung Thanh village. The report of enemy presence there, from which had arisen such excessive expectations, proved to be another will-o'-the-wisp or glittering mirage.

Therein the hope that failed typified this particular campaign in June 1966, if not the war as a whole. Little or nothing had worked out according to plan. Where the enemy was found, all of the circumstances suggest that there he was hoping and planning to that end. The only exception is Plummer's fight at the sugarloaf, where owing more to chance than to deliberate design, the Americans gained a tremendous advantage and the ambushers became ambuscaded. Otherwise, the battle had gone as if conducted by two sides, if not equally blind, then evenly matched in their awkwardness. The superabundant mobility of the Americans had enabled them to come up swiftly, and in some cases too fast. Most of their grief came of engaging precipitately while reconnoitering indifferently. The NVA and VC, on the other hand, were so intent on rigging ambushes that all else they did in battle was managed miserably.

On 25 June, the day after the shoot at LZ Apple, General Jack Norton redrew the boundaries for his forces. He was still convinced that the enemy was present in great numbers in the countryside east of Dong Tre. So on the map he plotted a line running from LZ Apple to the crossroads east of Trung Luong village where the artillery had based. Colonel Moore and a large part of his brigade would sweep to the north of it. Colonel John Hennessey and his brigade would flail out the countryside to the south of it. The southeast corner of the area remained a shooting gallery. Any chopper that flew that way was well worked over by the enemy AA guns. For this reason mainly, Norton's hopes stayed high. So on 26 June there was a great powwow at Dong Tre with all field commanders present. "If our information is right," said Norton, "every battalion ought to have a good target."

They went forth and they spent the rest of June beating out the countryside. Nothing came of it other than a few insignificant sightings of a few people in movement at great distance. Norton knew then that the enemy forces had donned black pajamas and conical hats, dissolved into small parties, and stolen away. The situation was exasperating.

In Norton's mind, thereafter, the campaign would be remembered as a freak accident. The enemy had intended only to knock off the CIDG companies at Dong Tre. The Americans had intervened in time to spoil that design and punish the perpetrator. To that extent, they had achieved surprise and won a victory of sorts. The published statistics supported that view. The friendly side had lost 66 KIA and 353 WIA. It claimed to have killed 423 North Vietnamese and 130 Viet Cong. The figures were probably conservative. From the figures, Norton drew a certain comfort.

There is another way of looking at it—that the enemy got what he wanted and that the attack on Dong Tre was only the first gambit in the setting of a very large trap. The NVA had chosen their battleground, with Trung Luong village at its center because of the maneuver advantage deriving from its tunnel system. All things done by the forces of the other camp, and in particular the fortifying of the ground most likely to be used for landing zones, reflects a decision taken much earlier to stand and fight.

HOA HOI, THE
THIRD BATTLE

JACK NORton's air cavalrymen were singing no September songs. They had spent the month afield in a great sweep called Operation Thayer that was supposed to purge the Soui Ca and other near valleys of the Viet Cong.

Now they were about to say good-bye to all of that, and happy day. Aside from fatigue and frustration, the campaign was without consequence. Though there had been frequent alarms and excursions, the birds had flown the nest. It was a grinding disappointment that turned troops sour. As September closed, there remained just a little tidying-up, a poking away at odd corners that had been missed by the big sweep.

On the morning of 2 October 1966, the task given Alpha Company, First Battalion of the Ninth Cavalry, held the promise of a routine surveillance, though "normal" is probably the better word for any operation by that unique fighting organization. The First does nothing routinely. The First has its own lift and fighting aircraft. It scouts the nap of the earth looking for enemy signs. Making contact, the First engages, and if the enemy force is too powerful, it blows the whistle and the Division sends help. The First's code name is Apache.

Set inland about twelve hundred meters from the China Sea, and a short walk east of Highway No. 1 that runs parallel to the oast, is the small village of Hoa Hoi, its neighborhood sweetned by a circlet of sleepy lagoons. At first glance one seeing Ioa Hoi from the air might mistake it for a fishing village, since river flows past its door to blue water. Yet it was a settlement f small rice-growing farmers and it looked as innocent as Maud fuller who raked the meadows sweet with hay. The scouting lements of First Cavalry Division (Airmobile) had not pre-iously bothered to give Hoa Hoi a passing glance, an oversight aat could hardly be charged to carelessness.

Tactically, Hoa Hoi had the nature of a dead end. With the road highway on one side, the sea on the other, and bare sand ats running from it north and south, the village afforded no onvenient escape routes. And at this season, the whole coastal lain was in flood due to torrential rains.

So when Major George W. McIlwain, the commander of /1/9, got the order from Division that he would run a recon n Hoa Hoi just to get it off the checklist, it seemed like one nore ho-hum assignment. At the main base, An Khe, and round the forward base at LZ Hammond, that is near the coast, he intelligence hands were all but convinced that neither NVA orces nor VC in any significant numbers were to be found in he near territory.

McIlwain (code name Apache Six) nonetheless hopped to it. t 0800, by which time the ground fog had lifted, three aircraft ook off from LZ Hammond, one scout party flying in an H-13, ollowed out by two armored UH-1's, or gunships. The pattern f employment was the accustomed arrangement, the scout ship lying the nap of the earth, either just over the treetops or at ifteen to twenty feet above the ground, and taking it just as lowly as possible. The gun team maneuvered around the scout hip in a two-to-six kilometer circle, remaining always within adio and visual contact.

In charge of the mission was the platoon leader, Major Joseph . Koehnke, thirty-two, of Alliance, Nebraska. Koehnke, slightly built and very blond, is a graduate of Omaha University. Though he talks in a very gentle voice, faster than a horse can trot, he seems to measure every word. His manner radiates self-assurance which with his personal warmth makes him that happy combination—a man worth following and a topnotch technician.

Koehnke's ship was formidably armed. The nose spouted M-79 grenades. There were the standard M-60 machine guns in the doorways, and on either side was a pod with seven rockets.

Koehnke and his gunship had just come even with the coast line and could see the scout ship barreling along just above the sands about two kilometers when over the radio came the first message from the scout party.

The words were: "Now over Hoa Hoi. See seven NVA. They have weapons. Are running for positions."

That was enough to get both gunships running for Hoa Hoi.

On his first pass Koehnke's gunners cut down seven khaki-clad figures while they were running for cover. The number is strictly coincidence. They could hardly have been the same seven seen by the scout ship. Too much time had elapsed.

Both gunships made three more strafing runs, saw no more live targets, and so far as the crews knew, killed no one else. Yet the air about them sizzled with bullet fire from the ground and Koehnke noted that the village was entrenched and bunkered throughout.

He called McIlwain to say: "Apache Six, I estimate at least a platoon in Hoa Hoi. [This was based on the amount of fire from the ground.] And definitely NVA."

McIlwain replied: "Am coming to you right now."

Said Koehnke: "And send another gun team."

Four minutes later Apache Six was over the scene. One quick look and he sent the order back to LZ Hammond: "Launch Blues on my location."

Koehnke and his gunships backed off to interdict any attempt at enemy withdrawal out of Hoa Hoi. Koehnke also thought of gistering 155-mm. artillery fires on Hoa Hoi out of LZ Hammond but decided against it because of the heavy air traffic.

Lieutenant Philip T. Lewis, Jr., was at LZ Hammond when he got the word to "saddle up." A resident of Plainville, Massachusetts, Lewis, twenty-four, had been a platoon leader for just four days. Within six minutes, he was airborne with thirty-two men, formed in four squads (three with six men, the other with seven), two RTO's, the platoon sergeant, one aid man, and a forward observer. A gutty little squirt, standing only five feet six and weighing 135 in his jungle boots, Lewis that morning had received a letter from his dear woman, a senior at Massachusetts University.

Lewis knew neither where he was going nor the mission. No time had been wasted in the giving and receiving of instructions. That would come after they got aloft—the customary procedure in this unit. They had scrambled aboard heavily loaded, each rifleman carrying 350 rounds for his M-16, 6 frags, 1 WP, and 2 smoke grenades. With the two M-60 machine guns went 2000 pounds.

Apache Six was on the RT as the last Huey took off, giving directions: "You are going into a village. One platoon of NVA is there. Your LZ is on the beach. Move off on azimuth of 270. Go directly into the village. Cut it in half, then turn and move south."

The LZ, already marked with smoke, proved to be fairly hard ground just off the sands. There were a few holes around it—foxholes—between the smoke and the village. On the other side of the LZ, low sand dunes ran eastward two furlongs or so from the smoke almost to the edge of blue water. If picturesque, it was nevertheless much too tight for comfort.

With Lewis in the lead, they made a four-ship touch down at exactly 0830, and so clocklike was the unloading that the four Hueys were away again in less than five seconds. There had been no fire. Within the next minute they had formed their

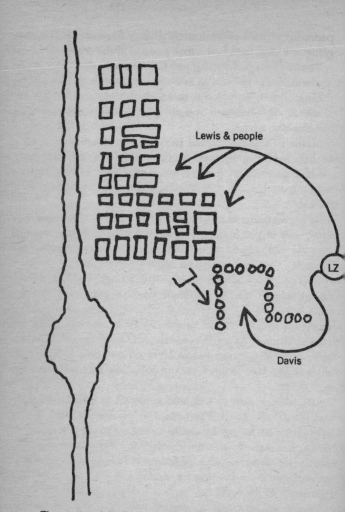

The scattered deployment of the Blue Team at the Battle of Hoa H

perimeter with an approximately seventy-five-meter radius, men going at a dead run. Lewis took position in the center.

The edge of Hoa Hoi lay just 130 meters to their west. Quiet at the moment, the village looked innocent enough, though the outline of the few huts was barely discernible at this short distance, so dense was the overgrowth of palms, vines, and other vegetation.

McIlwain, Apache Six, had landed right behind them, anxious to make certain there would be no mistake. Pointing to Hoa Hoi, he said to Lewis: "That's it. Move in. Cut it in half. There's seven Charlie dead in there. Pick up their packs."

Then Apache Six took off.

Lewis remarked to Sergeant James R. Petergal: "For now, let's think only of getting into the village." A Pittsburgher, Petergal was an old regular with twenty-two years of service. He answered: "That may take a lot of doing."

The newly landed men started forward in column of squads, not in single file, but well fanned out. Then halfway, they extended their front. Staff Sergeant Robert B. Davis, twenty-seven, of Mullins, South Carolina, was well over on the left of the formation. A Negro and airborne all the way, Davis is solemn faced, very black, and so reserved as to seem reclusive. In hours of dealing with him one never meets a smile. He may have deep fires but there is never a flicker on the surface.

Overhead a scout ship sighted two NVA in a foxhole twenty meters in front of Davis and the door gunner opened fire. The pilot of the Huey was vigorously gesturing, pointing downward. Davis got the idea; the pilot was signaling that he had knocked off the two Charlies. Davis, and Sergeant Ronald H. Mis, twenty-two, of Reed City, Michigan, a fire team leader, advanced cautiously.

The pilot had made only a slight error. Two dead men were slumped over the edge of the hole. Under them was a very live Charlie. He opened fire with an American carbine. The bullet stream went between Mis's legs. Davis charged the hole and dropped a frag grenade over the lip. The explosion took care of the third man. They recovered three weapons, badly beaten up. The bodies were dressed in khaki.

Ten meters farther on was another foxhole. A Charlie bobbed up like a jack-in-the-box, his AK-47 pointed at them dead on. Before he could press trigger Mis and Davis together put a dozen bullets in him.

Another enemy soldier stood in their path pointing an LP-40; the scout ship cut him down.

By this time they were flattened and fire was coming at them from three or four different directions. They crawled to the cover of a chest-high cactus hedge. Davis felt badly bothered; it seemed to him that the formation, or at least his squad, had been drifting much too far to the left, and such was the cross fire that he suspected they were going against an L-ambush. Looking to his right he could see no other Americans.

Three minutes of this and he called Lewis on the RT to ask: "Shall I pull back?"

Lewis said: "No, hold where you are, and be sure to pick up all VC weapons," a routine instruction in Vietnam that gets very tiresome.

Davis and his men were then about thirty meters from the nearest huts. They were adrift and Davis knew it.

Peering over the top of the cactus, Davis saw a fire-slotted bunker dead ahead, within easy grenade range. He threw a frag and it exploded next the baffle door. There emerged twenty-one women and children who walked straight past him, bound for the dunes.

"By God, what luck!" Davis said. "I didn't hit a one."

Behind them dashed a figure in khaki, sprinting for the beach. Davis shot him in mid-flight.

Davis rose again to grenade toward the bunker. Before he could throw, a Charlie jumped up from a camouflaged foxhole ten meters to the rear, his AK-47 pointed at Davis' back. Sergeant Mis got to his feet, facing toward the danger, his body covering Davis, and shot the man just in time. Then a second Charlie jumped out of the same hole, firing as he arose. The burst of bullets shot Mis through the stomach and chest.

Mis toppled over, seemingly dead, not saying a word.

Davis figured it would be suicide to reach for Mis at that moment.

Davis was beginning to feel mighty lonely.

He called Lewis again, to give him a quick rundown. He concluded: "Lieutenant, I think I got it under control but I'm sure drawing a hell of a lot of fire."

Lewis passed the fresh information on to Apache Six.

McIlwain asked him: "Do you know how many people are in that village?"

Lewis replied: "I haven't any idea."

He still thought, however, that he was fighting a platoon. It was another illusion, as was his belief that Davis was about fifty meters to his left. Davis, in fact, was putting up a one-man show more than two hundred meters from his closest help. It was just as well Davis didn't realize it.

The rest of the skirmish line formed by three squads was by this time approximately even or on a parallel with the cactus hedge covering Davis.

Lewis, about thirty meters behind the skirmishers, suddenly heard the rattle of many weapons to his immediate front.

PFC Jack Hideman, grenadier of the third squad, had almost stumbled over two NVA's who were setting up a .50 machine gun in a ditch. He was ten feet off when he saw them, which was much too close for a grenade toss. So he charged them, firing his Colt .45—and missed. The Charlies took off for the nearest hut. Hideman jumped for the machine gun. Sergeant Petergal and the squad leader, Sergeant Harvey L. Atkins of Austin, Texas, mowed down the two runners with their M-16's. A third

NVA came on the run from the far end of the ditch. A thump gunner, Spec 4 Laird, firing from the hip and aiming for the runner's stomach, blew his head off.

0915 and the fight had been going less than an hour.

There was heavy firing now somewhere around the extreme right flank. Lewis knew that his first squad lacked a radio. So he got on the RT to Sergeant Ronald L. Christopher of second squad, asking, "What's going on up there?"

Christopher, twenty-eight, of Evert, Pennsylvania, answered: "Sergeant Martinez [leader of the first squad] has run into another fifty [.50 caliber] machine gun. It's in a hooch and firing right down our front. We can hear BAR's and AK-47's firing from right around it."

Lewis said: "Get over to Martinez and tell him not to push too hard."

Lewis was now feeling a great doubt. If there were present two or more .50 calibers and all else he had already heard in action, he was not coping with a platoon and this was no time to push troops. He would stay where he was and think things out.

Davis had arrived at approximately the same conclusion. He was flattened as low as possible behind the cactus bank and making no attempt to fire. Bullets from several directions were buzzing overhead. But the earth bank that supported the cacti was stopping the grazing fire.

At just about this time Major Koehnke returned to the scenario, mainly because Apache Six's Huey was running out of gas and McIlwain was heading back to LZ Hammond. Koehnke flew over and what he saw became a picture retained in his mind thereafter.

Davis was flattened behind the cactus-topped embankment, hugging earth, and no other American was anywhere near his squad. Koehnke wondered at this. Davis was pinned beyond mistake.

Koehnke spoke to Lewis on the RT: "Do you know you have

a man out there with no part of your line anywhere near him?"

Lewis said: "That's news to me."

Koehnke's personal performance thereafter is deserving of the closest regard. In a very real sense, it was *his* fight. He had started the whole thing. Of his initiative had come the commitment of the Blue Team and he behaved as if he were carrying the full weight of the fight on his shoulders.

He made a run directly above the main/ stem of the village, keeping the Huey less than a hundred feet above ground. The M-79 grenade launcher in the Huey's nose blasted away throughout the double pass, firing almost a hundred rounds.

In those few seconds Koehnke saw much that Lewis and his skirmish line had missed wholly. At least forty to fifty khaki-clad figures were moving in the open beneath him. Some were in a solid body, moving southward toward the canal at the edge of the village. Others stood next the huts firing their AK-47's upward at him.

The most amazing sight of all—one NVA from a pit in the center of the village street was firing an 82-mm. mortar straight upward in a futile effort to bag Koehnke's chopper, possibly the only time it's ever been tried in war.

During the two passes, the Huey took seven hits by bullets, and Koehnke made up his mind that the Blue Team had bitten off far more than it could chew.

He called over the RT to Apache Six: "I am upping the enemy strength to one company. We need a reaction force. I mean we should have had it ten minutes ago."

Koehnke made another pass the length of the village, flying higher this time. He counted at least ten stilled forms lying in the street and credited his M-79 fire with the kills. Also, he saw for the first time a trench line along the eastern edge of Hoa Hoi, manned by about two squads of NVA who were actively engaging Lewis' skirmishers.

Over the RT, Koehnke heard McIlwain (Apache Six) say to

Colonel James Smith (Saber Six), the commander of the First of the Ninth: "We must have a reaction force. This is bigger than we thought."

Koehnke called down to Lewis: "You hold what you've got. Either pull the fourth squad [Sergeant Davis] over to you or you go to it."

Lewis answered: "We're drawing too much fire to make a move. Otherwise the situation is under control."

Just then, however, Lewis got this message on the RT from Davis: "Got a man here either KIA or WIA and I need some help." Davis was speaking of Sergeant Mis.

Lewis sent his forward observer, Sergeant Michael A. Villie, twenty-four, of Mitford, New York, and an aid man, PFC Elie Medlin, Jr., twenty, of Morrisville, North Carolina, scouting leftward to get to Davis and attend Sergeant Mis. They moved out at a crawl. Villie, who went along just to give the aid man some fire cover, was carrying his radio, which proved to be a mistake. The PRC-25 was shot from his back en route.

Davis, meanwhile, was getting this word from Koenhke: "Better see if you can ease back to the LZ."

Tied to his ground by Sergeant Mis's condition, Davis sent PFC Bobby R. Bryant, eighteen, of Wichita, Kansas, to reconnoiter a withdrawal route.

Bobby didn't get very far. A camouflaged enemy communications trench heretofore undetected, ran parallel to the path along which Bryant was crawling rearward. A pair of NVA skirmishers had worked down this ditch to a point on Davis' rear. Their AK-47 fire nailed Bryant right through the left side. Bryant sprang to his feet in his last moment of life.

Davis yelled: "Where in hell are they?"

Bryant pointed to the ditch, and still uttering not a sound, pitched over dead.

Medic Medlin came up just at that moment and, seeing Bryant fall, rushed to help him. From the same ditch came another burst f fire. Medlin was downed by a bullet that got him in the right arm and a grenade that exploded into his face.

First pulling Medlin to the cover of the cactus hedge, Davis called Lewis to say: "Now two of my men and the medic are hit. can't move because there's no way to get them out."

McIlwain, having refueled, was now back in the fight. He flew in very low and began dusting the ground on all sides of Davis with M-79 fire. Davis, otherwise flattened, kept waving his arms to show McIlwain where the grenades would do the most good.

By now another NVA .50 machine gun was bearing down on the right of Lewis' line of skirmishers.

Lewis called Sergeant Christopher on the RT to ask: "Can you knock out that gun?"

Christopher said: "I'll try."

From forward came the sound of numerous grenades popping off. PFC Lynn P. Gaylord, twenty, of El Cajon, California, had exposed himself momentarily to draw the .50's fire and get a fix on the position, about twenty meters off. Then the whole squad had grenaded together. But the enemy gun fired on.

In the next round, three NVA soldiers tried to make a sneak run around the squad's right flank while the sweep of the machine gun kept the Americans flattened. Private Gaylord charged them firing his M-16, killed all three, and returned to his position.

On order from Sergeant Daniel T. Martinez, twenty-one, of Clovis, New Mexico, PFC Lueck, a thump gunner, made his try at knocking out the gun. Getting off his second M-79 round, Lueck, twenty, of Glencoe, Minnesota, exposed himself just a bit too much and a .50 caliber bullet hit him through the left chest.

He said to Martinez: "I'm hit, sarge," and died. He had said it as quietly as if he were objecting to something only slightly unpleasant.

Seconds later another .50 bullet drilled Gaylord through the right arm. Gaylord's response was the weirdest kind of thing. He ran over to Christopher's squad, yelling: "We got a man hit [referring to Lueck] and we need an aid man right now."

Spec 4 James T. Jones, twenty-three, of Brooklyn, followed him back to Martinez's squad, and on discovering that Lueck was dead, joined Gaylord along the fire line. Gaylord still paid no attention to his own wound. Jones tried to bandage him, only to get shaken off.

Christopher had been studying the problem and moving his men about. He called Lewis to say: "I think I'm in position to get that gun now."

Lewis said: "Then you hop to it."

In three minutes of action, Christopher and his helpers put thirty-six M-79 rounds and eighteen grenades into the position. That blast killed the enemy gun and everyone around it.

Hearing the news, Lewis said: "Go in there and get that gun!"

Christopher replied: "Not on your life! Everything is still too hot up here."

It was then about 1000 and the fight had been going for less than three hours.

McIlwain was on the RT to Lewis, asking: "What's the situation?"

Lewis said: "We're in heavy contact. We can't go forward and we can't pull back."

By this time Lewis was feeling badly shaken up and he knew that his voice betrayed it. He was using the words of steadiness but they didn't sound right to his ear.

McIlwain said: "You take it easy; help is on the way."

With the assistance of his RTO, PFC Manuel Garcia, Lewis put out smoke grenades to mark the position for McIlwain's benefit. Koenhke, having fired every round of ammunition aboard his ship, returned to LZ Hammond to reload. Davis and the few people with him on the extreme left flank remained pinned down; not a man was firing.

NVA soldiers kept running past Lewis' front, bound for the

river at the end of the village. They were gunned down as they ran.

Sergeant Martinez had run out of smoke grenades. As a substitute, taking action for McIlwain's benefit, he tossed out a CS chemical grenade to mark the position.

The effect was astounding. A strong wind was blowing inland from the China Sea. It carried the gas into the huts. Out came the NVA, at least two score of them, dashing madly into the open, stampeded by a whiff of gas, spinning about with the eccentric motion of so many water bugs. Most carried weapons but they might as well have been clubs. None paused to fire.

Utterly astonished, Martinez yelled: "For God's sake, look what I did!"

Petergal was already up and firing his M-16 in a sweeping motion, full automatic. Lewis joined him. So did others, volleying without letup.

McIlwain's ship was just above the scene. The pilot, Lieutenant Patrick L. Haley, twenty-four, of La Salle, Illinois, dropped the Huey to thirty feet above ground and there it hovered. The two gunners, Specialists 4 Robert L. Andrews and Larry D. Wright, stood on the Huey's skids, raking the melee below with their M-60's. Wright, twenty-one, is from Centerville, Maryland, and Andrews, twenty-three, came from Perrysville, Michigan. Bullets from their machine guns kicked up sand within ten feet of where Petergal and Lewis stood. Such was the din, the clamor, and excitement of these three or four terrible minutes that nobody minded.

This heavy slaughter ended with the fall of the last khaki-clad target.

McIlwain's ship pulled off. There was a sudden quiet and momentary cooling.

Lewis felt such relief that he was shaking all over.

McIlwain called to him over the RT: "How are things going?"

Lewis said solemnly: "Sir, it was rough."

McIlwain replied: "I think it's time for you to back away from there."

Lewis glanced back to the landing zone as he reflected. The rest of his line could back off without trouble. But what about Davis on the far left flank?

Over the RT he said to Davis: "We're getting ready to move back."

Davis said: "Sir, I can't move. I got KIA's and WIA's. How can I move? I need help."

Lewis said: "We're on our way."

This was his plan. He would head for the landing zone, taking out the casualties from his own ground. Then he would take a party and try to extricate Davis.

The withdrawal was made without trouble. Lewis and his rescue group got halfway to Davis.

At that moment the problem was taken out of their hands. McIlwain, over the scene all the while, had been monitoring the whole conversation.

McIlwain said to Lewis: "I'm coming down to get Davis. Tell him to get ready to get the hell out of there. And you get the hell out of there also."

There was method in McIlwain's madness. First, his ship made a run directly on the enemy machine-gun nest, twenty meters to Davis' front, that had kept the fourth squad pinned down. In this pass, the door gunner, Wright, made a bullseye, killing one machine gun. Following in McIlwain's pilot, Haley, Lieutenant Robert D. Hurley, in another gunship, knocked off the second enemy machine gun. Hurley, twenty-four, is from Enterprise, Alabama.

Pulling out from that run, Lieutenant Haley orbited briefly, then in an approach so steep that it looked like a dead drop, put the Huey down on the patch of ground that lay between Davis and the enemy bunker.

The advent was so sudden that it "shocked and surprised the hell" out of Davis, to use his words.

Lieutenant James C. Schlottman, twenty-three, a Pittsburgher, artillery forward observer, stood in the door on the far side of the Huey, blasting away at the village with an M-60.

The gunners, Wright and Andrews, had jumped out. They were yelling at Davis: "Go for the ship! Run! Never mind your casualties! We'll take care of them."

But Davis didn't go for the ship. He lammed rearward as fast as he could run to join Lewis and the rescue party. The door gunners carried Medlin to the aircraft and within a minute the ship was away. The dead were left behind.

None of it was as easy as it sounds.

That the Huey again got airborne was a small miracle. In the brief time it had been grounded, it had taken multiple hits by bullets. As it gained altitude everything about the craft started failing at once. Haley kept it going seaward for not more than 150 meters and then the wounded bird gave up the ghost and went flop amid the sand dunes.

Heaven was still with this mission. Not a man had been hit.

Within a minute or so Hurley made his second strafing pass at the same target area, and that proved to be one too many. As he came out of it and circled back over the LZ, he heard a voice on the RT yell: "Hey, you're spilling gas all over us." It came from someone in the infantry below. Already aware that the Huey had been hard hit and possibly crippled beyond recovery, Hurley continued toward the sea and his chopper crashed, oh so gently, not more than two rods from McIlwain's wrecked bird.

All hands walked away from these wrecks. All were still whole-skinned. Guardian angels were also doing overtime duty.

Davis had just remembered something. He said to Lewis: "I left two POW's back there, dug them out of foxholes and then tied them up. Do you suppose the door gunners took care of them?"

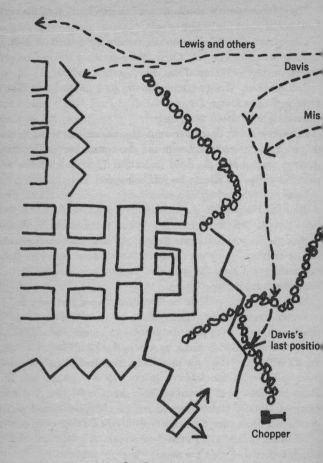

Lewis and others

Davis

Mis

Davis's last position

Chopper

Sgt. Davis at Hoa Hoi

The little lieutenant shook his head in wonderment at the ever-morose sergeant. Until this moment not one word had been said about POW's. Davis had been much too busy ducking bullets.

Another gunship pilot, Captain Lester C. Helmke, twenty-seven, of New Braunfels, Texas, flew into the dunes and dropped down next the wrecked birds. McIlwain quickly gave him a rundown on the last act of the withdrawal. The story stirred something in Helmke. He grasshoppered to the same spot where McIlwain had put down a few minutes before, and while he and his co-pilot covered them with the door guns, his crew scuttled about and collected the dead under fire. Then Helmke flew the bodies back to An Khe to be rubber-bagged. Heroism was quite common that morning and also fairly expensive. There were seven fresh bullet holes in Helmke's chopper.

Meanwhile another gunship, piloted by Captain Paul, lost power from taking too many bullets, and had to wash out in the dunes next the other two derelicts. "This place," Paul said as he walked away from it, "is becoming a little too crowded."

Koehnke, having gassed up at LZ Hammond, had flown back to Hoa Hoi. At Hammond he had looked his ship over and had counted twenty-three bullet holes—high score for the day. It cheered him that a Huey could be so resistant. Now aloft he heard a voice say: "I think it's about time we bug out to the east." With three gunships shot down and beached, he could but nod his head in agreement.

Schlottman and McIlwain couldn't get enough of it. They flew back to LZ Hammond where they picked up another gunship. Then they joined the afternoon fight at Hoa Hoi. In time their ship had spent all of its rockets and machine-gun ammo. But it did not withdraw from the area.

Schlottman killed one Charlie who was running for a trench, this with one bullet from his .38 revolver while the Huey was moving right along.

The incident reminds one of the anecdote about the Iron Duke in his stroll through Hyde Park. A stranger approached him and said: "Mr. Peabody, I believe." Replied Wellington: "If you can believe that, you can believe anything."

Back at the LZ next the dunes, while waiting to be lifted out to Hammond, Lieutenant Lewis was saying for the benefit of anyone who would listen: "I think we killed about ninety of them."

Nobody disputed him, and on the other hand, no one cheered. The truth is that not one of them had the foggiest notion of how the fight had gone as a whole. Each had seen just a tiny piece of it, the bit that took place on his immediate front or flank, his perspective being hardly better than that of a rodent. Whether they had been engaged by an enemy platoon or had taken on a battalion hardly entered their minds as a question. Each could say only that where he lay the ground seemed hottest of all. Yet the morn was fair and the sun not too glaring.

The reaction force—the greater part of one rifle battalion—had arrived at the dunes and was readying within calling distance. The Blue Team paid no heed and was hardly aware of its presence. There was almost no trading of information.

The newcomers rather took it for granted that the Blue Team had been too hard-charging, had gotten itself quickly compromised in consequence, and had then given up on a bad job.

Lewis and his people reckoned that they had all but shattered the NVA resistance and were leaving the larger force only the credit for what would prove to be a tiresome mop-up. Hence there was no good reason to review the situation. Furthermore, though Lewis and his team had been at grips with Hoa Hoi for the greater part of one morning, they still knew almost nothing about it. There had been no time to talk things over among themselves.

Both sets of assumptions were wrong, though these were not the only errors that came of this strange passage next the dunes with the inbound and the outbound behaving as if they were virtually alien to one another.

The new battalion saw the three wrecked gunships on the dunes, lying practically in line. Its men concluded that the ships had been flying in formation, and while so doing had been shot down by antiaircraft fire from the village, and that in this way the battle of Hoa Hoi was begun. One soldier said it to another, after jumping to a conclusion, and that's how the rumor got started.

Years later they would tell the tale this way and no one would be able to convince them that they were wholly mistaken. A good fable, once put in circulation, will always down the facts of the matter.

A STUDY IN COMMAND

ON THE MORN-
ing of 2 October 1966, Lieutenant Colonel James T. Root's battalion, the First of the Twelfth, was spread over much territory none of which gave forth a hostile peep. It was supposed to be screening and blocking while finding nothing to screen or block. Leaders and followers were bored stiff with it.

Charley Company was on the beach north of the village of Thanh Thuy. Alpha was at My Phu four klicks to the westward and over the coastal highway. Bravo Company was on a prowl in the jungle-clad range to the west of My Phu that Americans called the Crescent.

In one week of beating about, the battalion had wasted its energy without making a single contact. The mission, as it had been outlined, was to block on an east-west line from the mouth of the Song (River) Loch Li. Where the Song met the China Sea, the countryside was all salt flat, heavily inundated, and extremely marshy. Nearby was the southern flank of the Nui Meu Mountains, the hills and cliffs of which rose from the beach formidably steep and almost wholly bald.

Captain Frederick E. Mayer of Bravo looked at the Nui Meu heights that morning and said to his XO: "I cannot imagine a vainer mission than this: Charlie is long gone."

Mayer, thirty, from Norwalk, Connecticut, and USMA '58,

while not a perfectionist, has a reputation for undivided attention to duty. Though he tends to be overly concerned with detail, his men adore him because of his absolute fairness. At West Point he was regarded as an oddball because he would never deviate from a straight line.

Bravo's commander, Captain Harry T. Fields, would have agreed with Mayer's estimate of situation: They were on a wild goose chase. Fields is a more relaxed and quite casual soldier. He carries a shotgun over his arm in battle. His sense of humor is boundless, even when under fire. During Operation Irving, somewhat to Root's annoyance, he ran about with his trousers held up by a lacing from a jungle boot. Root finally gave him a belt.

As for James T. Root, USMA '45, he is the son of a National Guard captain who fought in Pershing's AEF in 1918. Robust, built like a middleweight, Root is a wholly congenial man who is at the same time intensely professional about fighting problems. Near the bottom of his class, he went infantry, and says he would have done it anyway, even had he been a whiz kid. Aged forty-three, Root lives in Carmel, California.

Root was flying in his TOC ship over the battalion area when at 0930 information came over the RT about action on the beach. It got to him roundabout through Colonel Archie Hyle. The were about as follows:

"At Hoa Hoi the Ninth cavalrymen have received fire."

"The Blue Team has been put down to east of the village."

"Before they landed three ships were shot down."

"The ships are on the beach, two Hueys and one H-13."

"The Blues have made instant, heavy contact."

"The village is heavily bunkered and trenched."

"The Blues were put down in the angle of the village because the ships were shot down there."

"They will develop the situation and protect the choppers."

"They are taking heavy casualties."

"They claim a body count of fifty." This at the end of one hour.

By that time Root was fighting to get his mission changed. He had heard Hyle say: "It looks as if this thing is getting too big for the Blues."

It was Hyle's idea to back up the Blue Team by inserting the Second Battalion of the Eighth, which was fairly well concentrated about three klicks to the north of Hoa Hoi.

Root said: "I want a piece of the action and I can get there faster with Bravo Company."

Hyle thought a moment, then said: "Show me how fast you can get in."

Ten minutes later the first choppers for the lift were in the air over the Crescent to pick up Captain Mayer and his men. Mayer took off without knowing where he was going. Mayer was airborne in the Huey and wondering what direction to take when Root gave him the mission. This is not unusual; it happens more times than not.

Root first described the situation on the basis of the sketchy and—though he did not then know it—highly inaccurate information that had come to him.

Then he said: "Giant Bird, you will land on an LZ that we will mark with smoke. You will assume opcon [operating control] of the Apache Blues and then continue the attack on the village."

Mayer asked: "Is the LZ secured?"

Root answered: "No, it's quite hot."

By this time the ships in Mayer's first serial were over the southern end of the Nui Meus, and Root, having barreled for the beach, was orbiting briefly while looking for the best place to throw smoke for the landing.

Root had only twelve slicks—Hueys—in which to make the move but there was still no indication that he would need the whole battalion to go against Hoa Hoi and he reckoned that he could slip in the rest of Bravo Company with a fifteen-minute turnaround out of LZ Hammond.

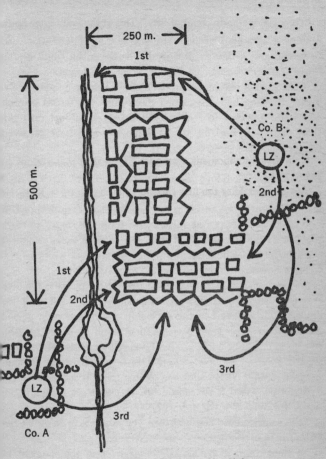

250 m.

1st

Co. B

LZ

2nd

500 m.

1st

2nd

LZ

3rd

Co. A

3rd

Movements of Root's Brigade at Hoa Hoi

The truth is he was feeling his way through the dark of an otherwise shining morning. His preparatory information had been bad and at least half wrong. Thereafter, he could get no direct contact with the Blue Team, either with Lieutenant Lewis or with anyone else higher up who could brief him adequately. So his thinking had been along these lines: He would commit Mayer & Company to feel out the situation but not do more than that. Judgment on any next move would have to await Mayer's report.

With Root in the command ship was his S3, Major Leon C. Biere, USMA '57, Root's "favorite smoke thrower." They orbited until they saw the first serial of Bravo's lift make the turn out at sea to begin the approach to the beach. Then they dropped to one hundred feet so that Biere could drop the smoke to mark the LZ. As the Huey hovered for a few seconds the air about it fairly buzzed with bullets.

Biere remarked dryly: "It's hotter than I thought."

Mayer was going in with only two platoons. The first five choppers carried First Platoon, commanded by Lieutenant Joe Anderson. Mayer was in the sixth ship. He had already passed the word to Anderson: "Apache Blue Team in heavy contact. We go in one klick north of Kay. LZ very hot. Friendlys between us and village." He now gave this same information to Platoon Sergeant Leslie Wilson who was coming on with Second Platoon.

Anderson asked: "You mean we should start spraying the wood line as soon as we're down?"

Mayer answered: "Yes, and then you come back to me at the CP." The same instructions went to Wilson.

As Root, from aloft, looked things over in the moment of touch down the Blue Team could be seen withdrawing to the southeast of the village. He saw "not more than ten men, moving slowly, carrying some wounded." Everything appeared rather vague. All that stood out clearly was the sight of two gunships, hovering over the village, not more than thirty feet up, blasting away with machine guns and rockets.

Mayer landed facing the China Sea. The LZ was an open sand flat about thirty meters east of the village, and at least that far north of the Blue Team's withdrawal line. First Platoon had already deployed a short distance to the westward and a few men were firing.

Mayer's first message to Root was: "We are catching a lot of fire, but I don't think we're getting hit."

Quickly Anderson and Wilson were with him and got their instructions. First Platoon would go to the northeast end of the village to "set up and block there and do nothing more." Wilson and platoon would stand by until Mayer decided where to lead them in person. His main worry in this first look at things was that the NVA would find an escape hatch and slip away, and as he saw it, their only chance lay to the north. Major Koehnke and the gunships were barring passage through the paddies to the westward.

Major McIlwain's ship landed on the LZ as Mayer completed his instructions.

McIlwain said: "Blue Team has three or four KIA. I'm pulling them out."

Mayer protested: "Blue Team belongs to me."

McIlwain replied: "Not according to my instructions." This closed the conversation. Mayer knew it would be useless to argue.

Lieutenant Walter Crimmins, the leader of Third Platoon, had come along on the twelfth Huey, just in case he might be needed. Mayer said to him: "Get ready to smoke up the LZ and bring your people along. We'll need them."

Wilson, not quite understanding what was wanted of him, had wandered off to vanish amid the trees at the southeast corner of Hoa Hoi. Mayer learned of it when he got this message from the platoon RTO: "We have linked up with Blue Team. They have quite a few wounded. Are withdrawing through us."

This was the only contact by anyone in the battalion with the Blue Team, and as to the amount of useful information the net result was zero. An absurdity, it happens all too often.

Mayer got Wilson on the RT and said to him: "Assault into the village."

At the same time, a message was coming in from Anderson, to north of Hoa Hoi: "No contact; no sweat; no nothing."

In this way had passed the first fifteen minutes. It took Mayer only that long to make up his mind that there was no way to "feel out the situation" except to fight. He was already moving obliquely left—southwestward—to join Wilson.

Mayer had given Root the information: "Blue Team is not opcon but leaving right now."

Root remained overhead.

He answered Mayer: "Let it go that way. To hell with it. Get on with the job."

Root was studying the smoke and all other signs while he puzzled about committing a second company.

Halfway to Wilson, Sergeant Major John Pearce, who was accompanying Mayer, threw out yellow smoke so that Root could follow their progress, of which there was very little.

Wilson had already given him pause with this message: "Don't come to me. I'm hung up in a trench system. I have one KIA [PFC Roy Salazar] and two wounded."

Mayer said: "Stay where you are and keep firing."

Wilson added: "Charlie is running around all over the place. And we're picking him off plenty."

Said Mayer: "Then don't move into the village. You'd just lose people."

Wilson said: "The action is all here."

Root, monitoring this conversation, made his decision to commit Alpha Company, also. But instead of committing it at LZ

Kay, one klick south of Hoa Hoi and next to the beach, thereby to block a possible escape route, he would deploy it against the southwest corner of the village. So he picked out a new LZ. Thus a tentative plan was scrapped when opportunity called. From what Wilson had said, Root guessed he was dealing with a demoralized garrison. Root was smartening by the minute.

Over the RT the order went to Captain Harold T. Fields, Jr., commander of Alpha Company. A twenty-eight-year-old graduate of the Citadel, Fields is from Orlando, Florida. Like Mayer, he had exactly 120 men in his outfit. The riflemen were carrying personal loads of 600 rounds for their M-16's, with 2 frag grenades. Every other man toted a claymore mine; and there was a like distribution of trip flares. With each machine gun went 1200 rounds; the thump gunners carried 40 grenades apiece. All hands carried three meals on their backs, along with two canteens.

These were simply hellish burdens, but there would be little walking, the temperature was not higher than 75 degrees and Fields could sense that his men were supercharged. The month-long frustrations over the failures of Operation Thayer had made them feel "lower than a snake's belly in a wagon rut." When Fields told them: "We got a target now, a real one, and no mistake," they actually stood up and cheered. Thereafter Fields's main worry was whether he could get them to the fire in time.

There were still only twelve slicks for the lift, so Fields set forth with his first two platoons and CP group. To save time, they were to come in on a new LZ, this at the southwest corner of Hoa Hoi. The serial missed the smoked LZ on its first try, roared directly over Hoa Hoi at fifteen hundred feet, circled out over the South China Sea, returned for a second try, and this time got the direction.

As the men scrambled from the ships they drew rifle fire at once. This was hot stuff, coming from snipers who had worked their way to a hedgerow-bordered hut a hundred meters away, directly to the north of the LZ. The men flopped down, volleyed for five minutes, and put an end to that. Later four NVA bodies were found along the hedges.

The Hueys had turned back, this time bound for LZ Hammond to refuel.

Fields called Root on the RT: "I'm here with two platoons."

Root told him: "It's your decision, whether to wait for the others or move now."

Fields said: "We move now."

Fields left nothing and no one on the LZ because he reckoned it would take the greater part of an hour for the rest of the company to come on. There would be time enough to get with that problem. The "company" moved out in two columns, each platoon sticking to a separate hedgerow, the men staying very low.

The point man of First Platoon, none other than Platoon Sergeant John O. Sinkovitz, was the first into the enemy trenches on the far southwest corner of the village. He moved right along, and as he came to the first bend in the trench, a bullet hit him in the thigh, broke the femur and hip, glanced off the bone, and came out on the inside of the leg.

Sinkovitz hardly staggered.

He propped himself against the trench wall, raised his M-16 and fired a long burst, killing not only the Charlie who had shot him but two men coming up behind him. Beyond them other Charlies were clawing their way up the trench wall.

Sinkovitz turned very calmly and said: "I think these punks are in panic."

They were. At least a dozen of them had jumped out of the works and were running for the line of the river just west of the village. Most of them made it. They dove in and wholly disappeared for a few minutes. How they managed it was at first a mystery.

Some of Fields's men had followed them out of the trench and were now flattened on the bank, peering toward the water, yet seeing nothing unusual. Most of First Platoon had stayed within the trench. From out of the river, several potato masher grenades sailed in on both of these groups. The grenades did no damage, but on the other hand, their source was baffling. The grenades seemingly had looped out of nowhere.

Where Second Platoon, following along, was coming up behind First Platoon and entering the trench, the river widened and formed a small lake. As the point squad came even with the west end of this water, three enemy mortarmen jumped from a camouflaged pit on the embankment between the Americans and the lake. One carried an 82-mm. tube, another carried the base plate. They were running straight for the water and they almost made it. Just as they got to the brim they were gunned down. The two men carrying the mortar pieces pitched on over into the water.

Someone yelled: "Why would they be doing that?"

Someone else answered: "There must be underwater caves all along the river."

It was a flash of inspiration, if a bit belated, and all hands got it very quickly. As the word passed up and down the line, Fields put it out over the RT to his two lieutenants, William Pritchard and Robert Robbins: "Put some men into the water!"

There weren't many volunteers and at first only two hardy souls, Specs 4 James T. Leva and PFC John Perry, dared it. They striped naked and dove in. There was a seven-foot drop from the edge of the bank to the water.

Leva, the first to finish his recon swimming, came up with a report. Still paddling about, he yelled: "There are holes all along here. They're loaded with VC. Throw me an M-16!"

By then Captain Fields had doubled back and come even with Leva. The chance taken by this one man shook Fields.

He yelled: "You come out of there!"

Leva replied: "No sir, I won't. I see a Charlie with a rifle

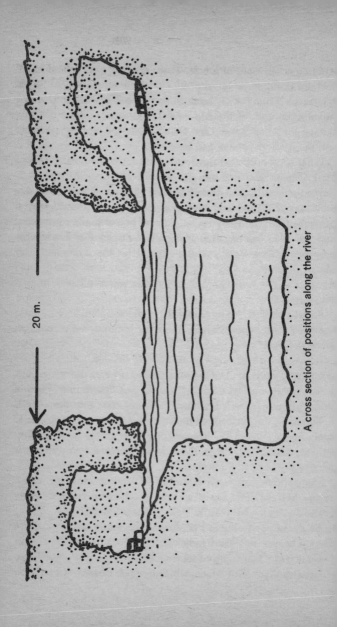

20 m.

A cross section of positions along the river

standing at the front of a hole. There are four men behind him."

Fields said: "Then you zap 'em all!" and pitched him the M-16.

Leva swam to the far bank, found a footing, and fired a full clip into the cave—man-made—on the other side.

That got Perry into the act. He swam for the target and began pulling out bodies. Leva had been right on the mark. Two of the Charlies were dead and three were wounded. All were clutching AK-47's. Perry swam on into the cave.

The entrance was at waterline. The chamber above the water-line was well aired and high enough to permit standing by a small man. Inside, Perry found a box of potato masher grenades.

While this went on, First Platoon had disposed of five snipers who had been tied into trees between the trench line and the village.

Fields called out: "We must get more men into the water." Twelve more men volunteered. They went in naked except for their steel pots, and they continued the probe of the caves along the bank for the next hour. Each platoon supervised its own water search, the extension of the front covering about three hundred meters.

By the end, their weird business along the river had accounted for forty NVA dead and eight wounded. There were fifteen caves altogether and the largest held fourteen NVA. One American had taken a slight flesh wound, the only casualty until then, except Sinkovitz. There is no accounting for the low American count other than through the manifest total demoralization of this part of the enemy force. It would not fight back nor could it surrender. Repeated attempts to get surrenders failed wholly. Most of the holes were attacked only with hand grenades.

The 82-mm. mortar crew that had precipitated this episode had been firing on Mayer's people at the southeast corner of the village. Mayer was in a trench at that point with his Second Platoon. The Third, under Lieutenant Crimmins, was coming up, along with Weapons Platoon, which had one 81-mm. mortar tube

and thirty rounds of HE. Crimmins was also in charge o
Weapons Platoon.

To Mayer's rear, not more than ten meters away, a morta
round exploded, its heavy crump well muffled by the loose sand
One frag hit Mayer in the lip, another got Sergeant Major Pearce
in the nose, and a third whacked PFC John Pelkey in the back.

Mayer was indignant. He felt certain that the round had come
from the 81-mm. mortar that was coming up with Crimmins.

He roared out over the RT: "Crimmins, stop that fire!"

Crimmins answered: "Hell no, it ain't mine."

But that answer didn't come over the RT. Crimmins was stand
ing only a few feet behind him, having just arrived.

Pelkey, an RTO, and former football star at Ohio State, wa
feeling no pain. Another RTO had lifted his shirt to see how
badly he was hit. The shard had penetrated, and its jagged
edge hung loose. The RTO pulled it out and handed it to Pelkey
saying: "Keep it for a souvenir." The wound still bled badly.

But after that first impulsive yell which shook out some of the
blood, Mayer found that he could hardly speak. He still fel
resentful toward Crimmins though he didn't know exactly why.

Maybe five minutes passed.

Out of the corner of his eye Mayer saw a mortar flash some
where near the river.

Then right at his back he heard another muffled crump. The
round had exploded not more than ten feet away from him.

Pieces of it hit Mayer in his right eye, upper right arm, and
elbow. One shard got Pearce through the biceps. Another struck
Spec 4 Knefle, the second RTO who had just done a favor for
Pelkey, in the right shoulder. Pearce had been hit while using
his body to shield PFC Jim Johnson, who was wounded earlier

Mayer blacked out for about thirty seconds. When his senses
returned, he was still in a foggy state. But he vaguely realized
that he had been harboring an undue suspicion. Crimmins wa
bending over him.

He said to Crimmins: "I guess nobody goofed; that couldn't have been our mortar."

Crimmins couldn't even get what he was talking about.

The round had caused two other casualties; the senior aid man, Spec 4 Wiseley and a rifleman, PFC Mazzola, had both been nicked, not enough to cry about, just enough to win Purple Hearts.

Mayer reported his own wounding to Root.

Root asked: "How bad?"

Mayer said: "Nick in lip, nick in eye, nick in arm, nick in elbow."

Root pondered a moment, then decided not to replace him. He sounded rational enough.

By then—it was shortly before noon—Fields's second lift, bringing the remainder of the company, was beginning to touch down at the LZ next to the dunes, and Root was making up his mind that the show was big enough, important enough, to call for the whole battalion, though only one forlorn platoon had gone against Hoa Hoi in the first place.

Captain Darrell Houston, commander of Charley Company, was chomping on the bit and asking for a piece of the action. Root said to him on the RT: "I'll drop over and give you a new mission." He was still not sure how he could employ another company to advantage right around Hoa Hoi.

Mayer's Second Platoon had become well set. The men had dug in, using only their steel helmets, which worked well enough in the loose sand. Heavy Weapons Platoon was directed to set up and register, but not to open fire. Mayer suspected that as things were going he would have to use its people most of the time to evacuate the wounded. He was still uncertain about where Fields's Alpha Company was deployed.

That doubt was cleared up by a call from Lieutenant Anderson, who had shifted First Platoon so that its line extended along part of the western side of the village.

Anderson said: "I have visual contact with A Company. They're about one hundred and fifty meters off. You can't believe what I see. They are fighting Charlie in the river. I mean they're right down in the water."

That call was abruptly broken off. Five NVA, two of them carrying machine guns, came on a run from the village, straight for Anderson's foxhole. Anderson quit the radio, picked up his M-16, and shot them all down.

Fields's turkey shoot in the water ended almost as abruptly. Or at least, his attention was drawn elsewhere. Lieutenant Donald Griggs, an Arkansan, had arrived with Third Platoon at the LZ southwest of the village which Fields had left unguarded and thereafter forgotten. The enemy had deployed another party to the hedge-bordered hut, this time with one machine gun and at least six AK-47's.

Fields heard from Griggs: "We are heavily engaged for now and can't get off the LZ. Will join you when I can."

The fight went on for twenty minutes or so. Griggs called back: "We have killed four of them. I have two wounded men. But we are moving." By this time, Fields and the men around him were also under intense automatic fire coming from out the village.

This quick enemy comeback surprised them. They thought that they had all but ended enemy resistance during the foray in the river.

Elsewhere the NVA was stiffening. At the southeast corner Mayer told Sergeant Wilson to have his men stage a "mad minute." Wilson did. For sixty seconds the Americans poured it on with all weapons. The sequel was three minutes of steady volleying by the NVA which kept all of Mayer's people pinned.

Root turned to one of the gambits in psychological warfare. Available to the battalion was a loudspeaker mounted in a Huey; the texts to be used during the pitch were rather standard stuff and already prepared.

At 1230 the ship was brought in. The announcement said that for forty-five minutes the Americans would suspend fire with all weapons. All civilians would be given the opportunity to leave the area and proceed to the open fields short of the beach.

Field objected to Root, saying: "I have all three platoons in heavy contact."

Biere replied for Root: "But you can't kill anybody till after the noon hour."

Fields asked: "But how can I get my guys to understand that when they're under fire?"

Fields couldn't even get the words that were coming from the tape, so heavy and persistent was the bullet swarm around him. He could see nothing but trouble coming from the experimental broadcast.

Nonetheless, it worked.

Old men, women, and childen started sifting out from the huts, quitting their protecting bunkers. At first they moved hesitantly and then they rushed, moving in four streams, to the south, north, and east; in the end they formed a pool of 171 souls to be evacuated by Huey from the beach, later to lead a forlorn life as refugees.

For Root's men it was an interlude in which they hugged earth, withheld weapons, and hoped for the best. The enemy continued firing.

Root brought Houston and Charley Company into a new LZ one klick to the northwest of Hoa Hoi. The company was 130 strong.

The mission as Root outlined it was about like this: "You will try to fix the limits of the NVA fortified area. You will keep moving through the several hamlets until you meet resistance. After that we'll see what comes."

It was roughly in his mind that he could form a pocket of Fields's and Mayer's soldiers, and Houston's men would serve as a broom, sweeping toward them. But the plan didn't work. Too many civilians were clustering around the fringes of the hamlets. The experiment with the loudspeaker had brought them out of the bunkers. Houston's men couldn't fire, but they stayed wide open to counterattack. When finally they got as far as the northern edge of Hoa Hoi, where Anderson's men had formerly been, they were crawling on hands and knees along the trenches and through the living quarters, hut by hut, and were accomplishing absolutely nothing.

Root set down in Fields's position, and so did Colonel Archie Hyle, the Brigade CO, whose numerous assignments in Vietnam have run the full range of dangerous duty. Together they sat on a log. For a minute or so they talked, reviewing the situation.

Hyle yelled: "Ouch!"

Root asked: "What is it?"

Hyle, who is as mild-tempered as a lamb, lifted his blouse. A grenade fragment had nipped the flesh of his abdomen. Such was the racket all around that Root hadn't even heard the explosion. The missile had come looping over from behind a hedge at their backs.

As Hyle doubled up, Sergeant Delbert Jennings, who had been collecting weapons, jumped through the hedge. A professional NCO from California, Jennings would later win the Medal of Honor in the fight at Landing Zone Bird.

Jennings' foot came down on the back of a wounded NVA lieutenant who lay there, an American M-1 carbine at his shoulder, its muzzle pointed at Root's back, a few feet beyond the hedge. Before the NVA could fire, Jennings killed him. For Root and Hyle this might have been a very close thing, though hardly a line soldier has served in Vietnam who cannot tell a similar story without stretching the truth. The number of hairbreadth escapes must be higher than in any other war. Or at least it seems that way to the veterans present.

Right after the clearing of civilians had taken place, and before any part of the stalled United States fighting line could get going again, Major Biere, who was still aloft in Root's chopper, asked Captain Mayer over the RT: "What do you have in mind to get things moving?"

Mayer said: "I'll put Anderson and his platoon through the village and then bring him over to me."

Anderson was willing and his people took off on a 160 azimuth, which is a little short of heading directly south. They moved in a skirmish line, using what is called "marching fire" (as prescribed by Georgie Patton) and throwing grenades as they advanced. Nothing much came of it, except that they again linked with the company. If there was any hurt to the enemy, it was beyond report.

Anderson's people almost got away with their sweep scot-free. At the last hut, Sergeant Jim Owens carelessly threw a grenade into a bunker. It was tossed back by a Charlie who escaped from a rear door in the bunker, and on exploding the grenade felled three of Anderson's men, though Owens stayed unhurt. Owens thought that was fairly amusing. The advance through the village had taken forty-five minutes.

On beyond Fields's extreme left flank on the west side of the village, an arched bridge spanned the river. Fields kept worrying that too soon night would fall, he would not have that small bridgehead in hand, and the NVA would use it in their getaway, toward his everlasting embarrassment.

So he ordered Second Platoon to cross over and keep the bridge secured on both ends. The platoon started, the point man, PFC Joe Cacgimble stepping off briskly. From a two-storied white house on the nigh side of the river, not thirty meters from where Cacgimble made the turn to start across the bridge, a machine gun opened fire. Cacgimble was killed instantly by a bullet through the head. The man who followed him, PFC Pipes, was shot through the lung, and the third man, PFC McDowell, after hitting the dirt, was drilled through the shoulder. The machine gun had stopped the advance cold.

Fields got his 90-mm. crew into the act, this from the night side of the stream, and with three rounds from that weapon the house was blown apart, including the three-man machine-gun crew. But Fields stayed less than content. A bunker next to the wreck of the white house kept bothering him. He figured there might be another machine gun within. He threw a red smoke grenade to mark it and idly hoped that some skyborne heavy weapon might come along to knock it flat. The morning had ended so auspiciously and the afternoon was wearing worse by the minute. The second machine gun continued to fire in short bursts; Fields stayed unsure of its location.

The complexity of the tactical problem was intensified by the layout of Hoa Hoi village. Until the gunships' fire had knocked down a large part of the overhang of palm and foliage that camouflaged the place quite effectively, the problem remained obscure. The village was shaped like an L, the base of which, turned toward the sea, lay along the river. Fields's men were deployed to the southwest and west of that base. Mayer's people were in an arc around the eastern end of it. The upper part of the L was by this time ablaze and smoke from the many fires blanked it out. The flames had neutralized that part of Hoa Hoi and driven the NVA resisters to concentrate in the base of the L, against which the Americans in the attack were packed too close for comfort. At the same time the conflagration had also virtually cut off all chance to maneuver. What to do was a puzzlement.

Mayer called for 155-mm. fire from LZ Hammond against the lower part of the village and the guns responded. One try at that was enough. The shells broke too close to his line and he could not adjust backward without risking ruin to Mayer's men. There just wasn't that much target area.

When Mayer called quits on the experiment, the ARA was brought on, four ships altogether. Their rockets exploded almost in Mayer's face, or so it seemed to him. Thereafter the fire against his sector fell off perceptibly.

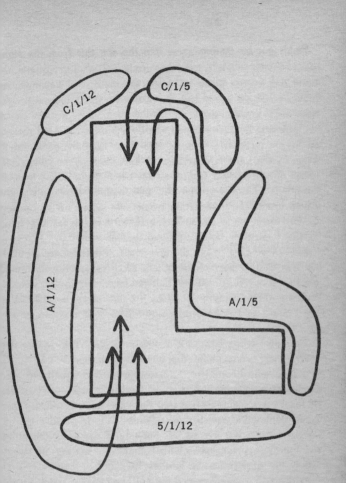

Positions and deployments in the Hoa Hoi sweeps as sketched by Col. Root

From above, Major Biere gave Mayer a fix on the bunker that was worrying Fields, for the one machine gun still chattered on. Biere did it once again by dropping smoke, and looking west Mayer could see the red plume distinctly, about 150 meters of right in the angle of the L.

Optimistic because of the damping effect of the ARA rocket on his own corner, Mayer figured that Crimmins could safely move by the right flank around the lower half of the village and knock out the bunker from the rear. Leaving one squad behind Crimmins took off with the rest of his platoon. It was a straight advance until they got within twenty-five meters of the bunker on the inner angle of the L. Then, as if on signal, fire came against them from both flanks and the line went flat.

PFC Steve Henderson, the first scout, was felled by a bullet. He was well in front of the others. PFC Francis Royall dashed out to rescue him. Royall got halfway back, carrying his burden and was there instantly killed by a bullet through the head. A third man (unidentified) ran to pull them both to cover; he was shot down.

Crimmins was putting all of this over the RT to Mayer. He said: "There's so much fire that we can't back away."

Mayer sent Lieutenant Anderson with two squads to give Crimmins a covering fire from "about fifty meters off" the base of the L. Anderson stepped into the same thing before his men could deploy and fire. Sergeant Owens, who had had a narrow squeak earlier, was creased on the side of the head, the bullet drilling through the back of his helmet after cutting the sweat band. The hit so concussed him that he babbled.

Both parties were flattened out and the move to knock out the bunker was at an end.

Mayer brooded, though not for long. Major McIlwain was again over the scene in his gunship, followed by two others. Getting the word from Mayer, they barreled one, two, three directly over his CP, going against the angle of the L, pouring t on with rockets, machine guns, and M-79 grenades from the nose launcher. It was a real smash and wholly effective.

While the impact was on, Crimmins and Anderson were able to back away with their people.

By then the day was wearing down and the light was beginning to fade, the hour being about 1730. Mayer was in no better shape; his wounds had taken a toll, his thinking was becoming fuzzy, and he realized that it was best not to go on that way. The two RTO's, Pelkey and Knefle, had made light of their wounds, but they had suffered badly from loss of blood. It was almost time for these three to get to hospital. The XO, Lieutenant David Pore of Kansas City, Kansas, would take command of the company.

Root was coming to a decision of another kind. He knew now that it was impossible to finish the resistance in Hoa Hoi before the dark fell without losing too many of his men. Though he had no idea how much force remained to the enemy, he would not accept an undue sacrifice of troops by attempting to close.

There remained the problem of closing all escape routes. That was easy enough during daylight. Though a full moon was in prospect, to seal off Hoa Hoi once night came, he had too few men. It was time to call for help, and not worry about the credit. A less solid commander than Root might have made a different decision.

Colonel Hyle, the Brigade commander, was at nearby LZ Uplift, the CP of Lieutenant Colonel Robert H. Siegrist, commander of the First of the Fifth. Root flew there.

He said to both of them: "I don't need a full battalion. Give me two companies. If Siegrist wishes to command, that will be OK with me."

Siegrist interrupted: "We'll be opcon to you."

Such boundless courtesy made one less problem for Hyle, himself a very gentle soul.

Ten minutes later Siegrist was on his way to his units. There

was one last touch of deference, Root saying: "You put them
in the way you see fit; so long as they are on my frequency, w
can work it out."

They had talked it over and agreed that both sides of th
perpendicular of the L, where the fires were beginning to bur
out, would be wide open for a breakout by midnight, unles
Siegrist's troops sealed them off. So fitting in the two companie
was a fairly simple operation.

The assignments were drawn by Alpha Company under Cap
tain George C. Shea, Jr., and Charley Company under Captai
Donald R. Sims. Within twenty minutes Alpha's 120 men wer
airborne in 23 slicks and Charley's 115 men were winging thei
way to the beach in 4 Chinooks. Sims touched down on th
beach at exactly 1900. Still, the last of daylight was gone by th
time the new companies had settled into the ground they ex
pected to hold for the night, and Root found that he had quit
a lot of adjusting to do.

The men from Siegrist's battalion had been deployed in a
rough semicircle around the north face and two flanks of tha
end of Hoa Hoi, with Root's men similarly formed around th
southern end in much the same positions they had held throug
the day. That allowed for a circle of foxholes around the whole
eight to ten meters apart, each holding at least two men.

But Root, now commanding on the ground, saw that the cor
don would not work. The trouble was that he had not enclose
the lake and it was essential to do so or any Charlie who mad
it to the water would get away. The moon was up, and he wa
also bringing in illumination, some of it provided by the 155's at
Hammond, and some of it from the flare ship, Smokey the Bear
The edge of the smoldering village was too near the water. Any
one could make a sneak crawl to it through the foxhole line. Bu
a swimmer would be seen on the shimmering surface. So there
had to be a widening of the circle and a general shift. By 2100

he inward-facing perimeter was at last locked in to Root's atisfaction.

The attempts to break out of the perimeter soon got started, ontinuing through the night. They came every five to ten ninutes and usually in the same pattern—parties of four or five NVA's trying to escape together, either by rushing suddenly or by crawling after one another.

In Crimmins' sector there was one variation. Crimmins heard a mooing to his front, saw six cows coming toward him (that they had survived the bombardment is astonishing) and guessed what was coming behind. His men let the cows pass, then opened fire, and five Charlies died.

As that fusillade ended, Crimmins heard two explosions just off to his right. He yelled: "What's it all about?"

Anderson yelled back: "I just grenaded two Charlies coming over me."

Root, who had bedded down with Alpha Company, was on the RT asking the same question. Crimmins was happy to give him the answer.

So it went. By midnight five small groups of NVA had made a run for the lake. They were all finished off in the water by Fields's men. In Sims's sector the getaways made their moves singly or in pairs. It made no difference. The night was kept bright enough so that they hadn't a chance.

Too many canisters from the 155 flares were falling amid troops. So Root switched to Navy gunfire illumination, than which there is nothing better.

Hyle wanted to cut off the lights, feeling there was too little payoff.

Root said: "Not on your life, our success comes of it, absolutely."

So the game went on, not unlike a shoot by British gentry in the Highlands, comfortably caped behind blinds, alert for the moment when the beaters would flush the birds.

There was a fifteen-minute shower at midnight, the only brea in an otherwise salubrious evening. It changed nothing at all.

The beaters, in this case the artillerymen of B/2/19, ke putting their fires on the main stem of the village. That nig they fired 862 rounds.

Frags kept flying into the foxhole line. Fields had three me wounded. Mayer had a medic wounded by this friendly metal

Shortly after the rain, Fields's people captured a wounde NVA medic who was trying to make a break for the lake. Th man talked all night; there was no way of stopping him. He sai that of four companies in Hoa Hoi when the morning began, a from the Seventh Battalion of the 18th Regiment, less than on company still survived.

That remnant stayed game. Around 0100, it staged a "ma minute." Root's people braced, expecting a rush to follow. I didn't come. If there was any such intent, it died under the retur volleying by Root's people.

Root had already put out his plan for the finishing-off opera tion when daylight came. The two companies from the Fift would attack from the north of Hoa Hoi and sweep on throug to Root's Alpha and Bravo. The four companies would then fac about and sweep from south to north.

The jump-off was at 0600 and the last act went slick as whistle.

Sims's and Shea's men on the down sweep drew no fire though they picked up six prisoners. On the back sweep, t everyone's surprise, Houston's company, which had drawn blank most of the way, had a chance to come even. It ran int a hard-core pocket of NVA diehards who were holding out in camouflaged trench.

The fight lasted four hours. Forty-one NVA were killed on thi ground. Houston did not lose one soldier. And when he returne with a grin on his face to join the battalion, his men wer escorting thirty-one NVA prisoners.

The other companies in the back sweep could claim a body count of ten. At least half of these had tried to hide away in small stacks of rice straw. Before the sweep was over, troops had grenaded into every hole and burned every hut and shed.

By 1230 on 3 October, the thing was finished. Where Hoa Hoi had been there lay only ashes, blackened spars, and uprooted, filth-covered vegetation, along with bits of stinking flesh.

BY WAY OF
POSTLUDE

O

THER SWIFT

sure successes for the Division, all along the seacoast, came quickly on the heels of Hoa Hoi. In the next few days was racked up a score truly impressive. Helped by the flooding of the tidelands, the Division made great gains with little loss.

Out of the heightened enthusiasm, it was decided to have another go at the Soui Ca area, this time on a limited basis, with no blowing of horns.

The reasoning was elementary. A division mount-up and shift in that direction would not escape the notice of VC scouts on the hills outside of LZ Hammond. Yet the chance existed that the Charlies would have thronged back into the three Binh Dinh valleys after the Division had cleared the area. By this time the Division knew that the CIDG Company at the foot of Crazy Horse Mountain (a unit described at length in my *Battles in the Monsoon*) had been penetrated by Viet Cong agents. It was considered likely that these agents had warned the VC in Soui Ca, 506, and Kim Son that the big blow was coming.

This time the task was given to Colonel Siegrist's battalion of the Fifth, and most of the workload fell on Bravo Company which had just been taken over by Captain James Taylor. The unit was lifted to the Soui Ca Valley on 8 October in Chinooks there to take over from A/1/12 commanded by Captain Darrell G. Houston.

While the assignment was an accident of numbers, it looked like an inspired choice. Within the battalion, leading the Second Platoon of Alpha Company, was a twenty-two-year-old Wisconsinite, Lieutenant William McCann. Operation Thayer had brought no laurels to the Division. Still, it had made McCann a figure of importance. He had proved to be the ablest searcher of them all. Of the thirty-three major finds made by all forces, and here we speak of stores rather than troop bodies, McCann had been responsible for almost half.

McCann called it luck. His mates knew it was not luck. McCann had served in Vietnam earlier as an EM, a chopper crew chief, and he knew Viet Cong ways so well that he could smell things out. Just prior to Operation Thayer, he had returned to the unit from hospital, after a protracted bout with malaria contracted in the Chu Pong Mountains next to the Cambodian border.

Still devitalized by that tour, McCann was outwardly imperturbable.

He had completely won his platoon. At every morning's start he would say to his men: "This will be the big one; we will make it bigger than ever." And the strange part of it was that the platoon always did. So he became idolized, though hardly an idol.

The platoon sergeant, SS Leroy Belfield, a twenty-three-year-old Negro from Norfolk, became entranced by him. He said: "The man's a charmer. He wants nothing but the best. So we're all for the best."

McCann's way of operating on search and destroy was to split the platoon into working parties of four men and deploy the groups checkerboard fashion, thus covering a tremendous amount of territory. Since there were not enough PRC-25's within one platoon to assure easy control of that many well-separated elements, he worked out a scheme for signaling within the platoon by firing rifle shots, a sort of boiled-down Morse code. This put a large trust in the judgment and steadiness of his squad and fire team leaders and they responded.

He grew endeared to them, however, above all else, because he was a workhorse. Despite his semi-convalescent state, he insisted on carrying the heaviest loads of any man present. When his men at times complained they were being overburdened, this jolly, not-so-green giant would laugh and reply: "Now, just watch me!" And his great body could stand the strain. McCann stood six feet, three inches. His soldiers had a pet name for him: Horse.

The story of this extra outing on the heels of Thayer-Irving is worth telling because of this one man, and also because its frustrations and small achievements typify the hopes and disappointments of the larger effort in September.

Moving his company by bounds, Taylor marched the length of the Soui Ca Valley, some twelve thousand meters, in five days. One rifle platoon stayed behind, covering the mortars. Two rifle platoons advanced abreast to extreme mortar range, with the 81-mm. fires rolling ahead of the line. The two rifle platoons then went into perimeter until the mortars could be brought forward.

By the end of the march, Taylor had come to the village named Hoi Son 5 (described in my *Battles in the Monsoon*). Almost nothing had been accomplished. On the third day the forward line flushed a VC squad. They were chased for half the day by half a platoon; there was a continuing exchange of fire at long range. No blood was drawn.

Even before reaching Hoi Son 3, on the fourth day, Taylor had noticed that his men were slowing down badly. The search of that place yielded only three tons of rice and a dozen NVA uniforms.

Came then a message from Third Platoon: "We have found

nother village in deep jungle; have seen about thirty VC of
nilitary age."

That proved to be the overstatement of the week. Taylor went
long as he moved up Second Platoon. The VC of military age
ad vanished into thin air. In the seven houses there were only
welve Vietnamese, all senior citizens.

Search of the houses, however, yielded a major find. Included
with the stores located among the ancients were six tons of rice,
ix NVA packs, two uniforms, five hundred pounds of salt, ten
undles of pongi stakes, and six hundred pounds of freshly-cut
eefsteak.

Taylor fairly whistled when he saw this trove, especially the
tore of fresh meat, more than enough to feed a hungry battalion,
hough the village had no refrigeration or any other means of
reserving it.

"Must be all VC here," said the ARVN interpreter who had
ccompanied him. "Must be troops somewhere near. Must be
lenty VC."

"That, my friend," said Taylor, "is hardly an inspired deduction."

Over the RT, Taylor asked higher command for permission to
urn the village, after evacuating the oldsters.

The reply was: "You may evacuate the people. You may
estroy the village. But you are not to burn it."

This sensitivity to public opinion back home and the MACV
trictures against atrocities in any form made the destruction of
he village a major labor. The supports of the buildings had to
e axed through. The banana and coconut palms were chopped
own. Thirty-six pigs were slaughtered. The rice was man-
andled and dumped into a nearby creek, where, rapidly swell-
ng, it formed a dam that wouldn't yield to hand grenades.
Taylor learned that there is only one easy way to destroy rice;
erve it with chop suey.

While the work went on an LRRP (these long-range patrols
re nicknamed Lurps) from the battalion, under Sergeant

Thomas A. Campbell, twenty-three, of Honolulu, passed through Taylor's position. With only three other men, Campbell was bound for the village of Hoi Son 1, but had been moving on route paralleling Taylor's running along the western side of the valley. His prosaic mission was to locate a suitable place to set up a battalion CP, and despite the weakness of his party he was breezing along with the breeze.

At the extreme northwest corner of the valley, the growth on both sides becomes so dense that the foot traveler has no choice except to take the low road and move directly on Hoi Son 1. So Campbell found it. The jungle denied him any alternative.

As he entered the village, the twenty or so Vietnamese who were lounging along the central path began clapping and talking loudly. From the broad grins on their faces Campbell thought he was getting a royal welcome. Then the clatter loudened and he realized it was a signal.

The patrol rounded the corner of the first house. Campbell saw an old woman running, bound for the third house. The four men raced her to the building, and she won by a few strides. As they broke through the door, a squad of NVA that had been at lunch crashed the rear wall. Blindly Campbell fired a quick burst, then ran outside the building. The targets had vanished.

The patrol collected the people of the village and had them lie face down in the central path. Campbell knew they were VC sympathizers, though he had yet to learn that the fifty-five-year old female who had outrun him was the political organizer and liaison agent for the Viet Cong of the valley.

Next, he called Taylor on the RT to tell him: "I'm in a fight up here."

That was a little white lie but Campbell wanted help in a hurry, lest the VC squad double back, reinforced.

Taylor broke off work and rushed the two rifle platoons forward.

The destruction of Hoi Son 1 began with the firing of an M-79 round into a thatched roof. Then the artillery was called on to work it over with white phosphorus shells, this being done by the eight-inchers of the 13th Field.

In the end all five of the Hoi Son villages were wiped out. The cattle were rounded up, 116 head, and a Popular Force unit was dropped near Hoi Son 1 to drive the stock from the valley for disposal by the district chief.

In the other company, Lieutenant McCann had started his last day in characteristic fashion, telling his platoon and his captain, George C. Shea, Jr., that he would make it a big one.

The first village that any of his men got into looked like a small fort to Sergeant Robert L. Burns of Charleston, West Virginia. The houses were log walls, fire-slotted. The entrance ports were too small for an American to squeeze through. Each house had a thick-walled protective bunker.

McCann had gone along with Burns. A woman, probably about thirty-five, was the sole occupant of the village. She was singing while she worked, stirring away at an enormous kettle which bubbled with enough rice to feed a company of men. On a table was a bowl holding several gallons of fish sauce.

She smiled at them and continued singing.

"What do we do about her?" asked Burns.

"Just let her keep on singing," said McCann, "she seems to be very happy."

At the third village of that day, they struck it rich. One squad under Sergeant Matthew B. Ware came to a building that looked ordinary enough. The exterior was of sheet metal siding and there were no windows. Inside, it was loaded with hospital stores, fourteen hundred bottles of penicillin, and great quantities of gauze, morphine, plasma, and bedding, the most valuable find of the entire sweep.

In another part of the village, a still larger warehouse was found to be loaded with sewing machines, ammunition, weapons and farm tools.

McCann's luck was still running and everybody felt good about it. The company had reached the end of the line and would have no more of the Soui Ca.

The campaign was over, the whole of Thayer-Irving. The battalion had been in the enemy valley more than one week and had done well. It had encountered no resistance except enemy booby traps, hand grenade-loaded, with a loss of three men wounded and none killed.

The column formed and the march started toward the nearest flat place in the valley from where its people could be lifted out for return to An Khe. As the head of the column approached the trench of the Soui Ca, following a path that wended through head-high field of elephant grass, Lieutenant McCann, who was in the lead, saw a fresh blood trail on the dirt of the path. It led into the elephant grass.

McCann called back to the others: "Hold where you are for just a minute!" then disappeared into the elephant grass. Several enlisted men, including Belfield, followed him at once, though he had not asked their help.

He had gone too far and too swiftly on this oblique move for the others to be with him when the thing happened. There was a sudden burst of AK-47 fire. Men still on the path heard McCann cry out: "Don't come in here!"

It was already too late.

Sergeant Ernest Pryor, right behind him, was down from wounds. Two bullets had hit him in the chest.

Spec 4 Horowitz, the aid man, had been behind Pryor. He lunged forward as he heard McCann call out: "Medic! Medic!" A bullet hit him in the right side, too close to the heart, however, and he quickly died.

Belfield got there in time to count the cost without being able to do anything to offset it. The VC were gone. They had made a bower by weaving together the overhead elephant grass that hid them perfectly. One pack had been left behind. The wounded man, if such there had been, had gotten away. Belfield could tell from the flattened grass within the blind that there had been three Charlies.

Sergeant Burns came up in that moment, Burns who later said that he loved McCann like a brother. Belfield stood there transfixed. The shock of seeing McCann down had been too much for him.

McCann was trying to talk. Burns bent over and got his words: "Don't bother about me; go after them."

Burns passed along McCann's words to Belfield, and then added: "We might as well do what he says. The Horse is on his way out. We can't do a damned thing for him."

Belfield said: "Dear God Almighty, don't let it be."

Three or four other men had come up to them. There would be company for McCann. So Burns and Belfield leaned to their task.

The two sergeants, both regulars, plunged on into the elephant grass. Unnoted until they stepped off, a narrow side trail wound from the rear of the ambush toward the flooding Song Soui Ca. Burns had taken special notice of how the Charlies had carefully plaited the elephant grass that curtained the blind so that the concealment was almost perfect. Hours of work had gone into the preparation. Worthless except for the one object of killing a man at point-blank range, it was something new in Burns's experience—a highly personalized deadfall. The thought of it made him shudder.

Burns and Belfield did not have far to go. Within less than three minutes they were at the river bank. Clearly uncrossable, the Soui Ca was a raging torrent, made so by the recent typhoon rains. That way there had been no thoroughfare for the three Congs who had shot McCann.

They knew then that the VC had sideslipped through the sea

of grass in making their getaway from the blind. So Burns and Belfield doubled back. Still, as they searched the ground just to the rear of the blind in trying to find a new lead, there wasn't the slightest sign of a blood trail anywhere around. The blind itself was unmarked.

So that was it?

Burns nodded to Belfield who nodded back. They didn't have to express their thoughts, which were bitter as bile. The blood trail that had lured McCann had to be a fake, a contrivance, very probably the blood of a slain animal, and hence the most ingenious touch of all. If so, there had never been a wounded VC. The trap had been rigged from first to last.

Belfield and Burns stayed silent. Their discovery that it had all been a mistake, they did not discuss with one another or pass along to the company. If it was a business badly done, it probably could have been done no better.

The play went on to the numbing and inevitable end. Horse McCann died as the stretcher bearers were lifting him to the medevac ship.

Behind him he left a sorely stricken outfit. One hour earlier, as these men had approached the LZ for their lift-out, they had been buoyant with the knowledge that they had not only survived but had made a high score and they had congratulated one another on a job well done. Now a sense of leaden futility weighed on their spirits. In some measure they were blaming themselves, and they felt resentful of a life that must express its values in terms of movement, action, and violence.

The company skipper, Captain Shea, said aloud: "This morning McCann said to me, 'I have been the luckiest man alive, but if I keep going I will get it.' Just why did he have to die?"

The others said nothing. To such a question there is never any sensible answer.

Soon they were airborne and the Hueys were heading for An Khe.

GLOSSARY

A-1E—U.S. Skyraider attack aircraft.

ADC—Assistant division commander.

AF—Air Force.

AK-47—Soviet assault rifle. AK is for *Avtomat Kalashnikoff*, or Kalashnikoff automatic, after its designer.

ALPHA—The letter *A* in the phonetic alphabet. The regulation spelling of *Alfa* is universally ignored.

ARA—Aerial rocket artillery.

ARVN—Army of the Republic of Vietnam. Pronounced *Arvin* when applied to a soldier of the ARVN.

ARTY—Short for Artillery.

AT—Antitank.

BAR—U.S. caliber .30 Browning automatic rifle. Replaced by M-16.

BLUE TEAM—Rifle platoon with UH-1 transport helicopters. Red team is two UH-1 armed helicopters; White team is DH-13 scouts.

BOONIES—Short for *Boondocks*, or "out in the sticks."

BRAVO—The letter *B* in the phonetic alphabet.

C-130—U.S. Hercules cargo-transport airplane.

CARIBOU—U.S. C-7 cargo-transport airplane.

CBU—Cluster bomb unit.

CHARLIE—The letter *C* in the phonetic alphabet. Also applied to Viet Cong.

CHINOOK—CH-47B transport helicopter.

CHOPPER—Soldier's term for helicopter.

CIDG—Civilian Irregular Defense Groups; local hamlet militia.

CLAYMORE MINE—Antipersonnel mine which throws out 700 steel balls in an arc of some 60 degrees. Lethal range is about 50 meters.

COMMAND BIRD—Aircraft in which a troop-unit commander circles a battle area to observe and direct his troops. Also called C&C (command and control).

CP—Command post.

CS GRENADE—Tear gas grenade.

DELTA—The letter *D* in the phonetic alphabet.

DSC—Distinguished Service Cross.

DUSTOFF; DUSTOFF CHOPPER—Evacuation of casualties; and the helicopter used for it.

81—Short for U.S. 81-mm. mortar.

EM—Enlisted man (men).

F-4C—Phantom fighter airplane.

FAC—Forward air controller; an officer of the air control team who, from a forward position aloft, directs the action of aircraft engaged in close support of ground troops.

FO—Forward observer; usually an artilleryman, he accompanies infantry and observes and adjusts artillery fire by radio or other means.

FRAG; FRAG GRENADE—Fragment; fragmentation grenade.

G2—Intelligence officer on the staff of a division or higher headquarters.

G5—Civil affairs officer on the staff of a division or higher headquarters.

GI—Term applied to the American soldier, carried over from World War II. GI = government issue.

GREEN BERETS—Popular name for Special Forces troops, because of their distinctive headgear.

H-13—Sioux observation helicopter.

HE—High explosive ammunition.

HQ—Headquarters.

HUEY—UH (utility helicopter), work horse of the Vietnam war. The name arose from the former designation of HU (helicopter, utility).

JCS—Joint Chiefs of Staff.

KIA—Killed in action.

KLICK—Soldier's term for kilometer.

LP—Listening post.

LRRP—Long range reconnaissance patrol.

LZ—Landing zone.

M-1 CARBINE—U.S. caliber .30, replaced by M-16 rifle.

M-16—U.S. caliber 5.56 rifle; the infantryman's personal weapon.

M-60—U.S. caliber 7:62-mm. machine gun.

M-79—U.S. grenade launcher.

MACV—Military Assistance Command Vietnam; highest U.S. advisory body to the Republic of Vietnam.

MEDEVAC—Short for medical evacuation. See also Dustoff.

MEDIC—Medical aid man.

MH—Medal of Honor.

NAPALM—Jellied gasoline used in flame throwers and bombs. From *Na*phthenic and *Palm*itic acids.

NCO—Noncommissioned officer.

90-MM.—Artillery piece, usually mounted on tank chassis.

NV(A)—North Vietnam; North Vietnamese Army.

105—Short for 105-mm. howitzer.

155—Short for 155-mm. howitzer.

PFC—Private first class.

PHANTOM—U.S. F-4 fighter airplane.

PIO—Public information officer; deals with newsmen mostly.

PF—Popular Forces. Native military forces locally recruited, employed within their home districts and organized into platoons. Technically controlled by district chiefs.

POW—Prisoner(s) of war.

PRC-25—Portable radio set, borne on a soldier's back.

RECON—Reconnaissance.

RF—Regional Forces. Native military forces recruited and employed within a province, organized into companies. Technically controlled by province chiefs.

ROGER—In radio language: "OK," or "I understand," or "Will do."

RPD—Soviet caliber 7.62-mm. light machine gun.

RPG—Soviet rocket-propelled grenade.

RT(O)—Radiotelephone (operator).

S3—Operations officer on the staff of a brigade or smaller unit.

SAPPER—Soldier who erects or attacks fortifications; usually one trained in use of demolitions.

SATCHEL CHARGE—Explosive package fitted with a handle for easy handling or throwing. So called because of its resemblance to a satchel.

SCREAMING EAGLES—Nickname of 101st Airborne Division.

SCUTTLEBUTT—Idle talk; rumor.

SF—Special Forces; also called Green Berets for their distinctive head gear.

SITREP—Situation report.

SKS—Soviet 7.62-mm. carbine.

SKYRAIDER—See A-1E.

SLICK—Unarmed helicopter or airplane.

SMOKEY THE BEAR—Smoke-laying helicopter or airplane, also used for dropping flares.

SPEC—Specialist.

SS—Silver Star.

THUMP GUN—M-79 grenade launcher.

TOC—Tactical operations center.

TOT—Term used to describe the method of artillery firing in which various artillery units so time their fire as to assure all projectiles reaching the target simultaneously.

20-MM.—Short for 20-mm. "minigun" carried in some aircraft. It can fire up to 4,000 rounds a minute.

VC—Viet Cong. In the phonetic alphabet: Victor Charlie.

WIA—Wounded in action.

WP—White phosphorus grenade.

XO—Executive officer of a small unit; corresponds to chief of staff of a large headquarters.

INDEX